YOUR
PUTTING
SOLUTION

ALSO BY JAMES SIECKMANN

Your Short Game Solution

YOUR

PUTTING
SOLUTION

A TOUR-PROVEN APPROACH TO
MASTERING THE GREENS

JAMES SIECKMANN
WITH **DAVID DENUNZIO**

Original photography by **Angus Murray**

AVERY
an imprint of Penguin Random House
New York

an imprint of Penguin Random House
375 Hudson Street
New York, New York 10014

Most Avery books are available at special quantity discounts for bulk purchase
for sales promotions, premiums, fund-raising, and educational needs.
Special books or book excerpts also can be created to fit specific needs.
For details, write SpecialMarkets@penguinrandomhouse.com.

ISBN 978-1-59240-907-5

Printed in the United States of America
1 3 5 7 9 10 8 6 4 2

Book design Tanya Maiboroda

To Michele, Hannah, and Samuel;
you fill my life with love and inspire me to do better.

Contents

Acknowledgments

During my younger days, I dreamed of playing on the PGA Tour, filling TV screens across the country with images of me holing putts and raising major trophies. But God Almighty had another plan for me— he knew my calling, selected my path, and deserves all the praise and glory. My blessings as a husband, father, and coach are immeasurable. I love what I do and can't wait to take on the challenges and opportunities that each teaching day holds. Oddly, doing what I can to help others achieve their playing dreams—whether it's one of my professional clients winning a tour event, an amateur player earning an athletic scholarship, or one of my academy students holding the member-guest trophy—has been more fulfilling than any fleeting success I enjoyed as a pro.

The best part of being a coach and a golfer is clearly the great people I meet every day. Thank you to my many loyal clients and friends—I truly appreciate your trust. I owe a special thanks to my first pro student, Tom Pernice, Jr., who is a short-game genius and ardent supporter. Tom, you have a huge heart and I clearly wouldn't be where I am today without you.

Thank you to Dr. Greg Rose, co-founder of the Titleist Performance Institute; Steve Shanahan, owner of Shadow Ridge Country Club and godfather to my first born; and Ben Crane, Cameron Tringale, Charley Hoffman, Kevin Chappell, Charlie Wi, and all the PGA and LPGA Tour players who have given me their trust and loyalty. I appreciate each and every one of you.

I've received a tremendous amount of support from other coaches, many of whom have become close friends. Thank you for your willingness to share your thoughts and embrace my message. I am humbled by your friendships and support.

Special thanks to my editor, David DeNunzio—you have a true gift for prose and composition as well as great taste in music. It's amazing that every lyric in every song rhymes with "DeNunz." It was enjoyable having you by my side.

Foreword

J ames Sieckmann has been my short-game coach since the summer of 1996. It's rare for a Tour player to have an uninterrupted twenty-year relationship in the golf business, whether it's with a manufacturer, trainer, caddie, or coach. We've both worked hard and have been good for each other. We both know how challenging golf can be. It hasn't always been easy for me—I've had some trying times as a Hogan (now Web.com) Tour, PGA Tour, and currently, Champions Tour player. Despite the struggles, I've carded six professional victories, and I owe a large part of this success to my relationship with James. Regardless of where I am or how I've played, James has always been someone I can rely on.

I'm excited that he's sharing his putting concepts with you, because it's so easy to get distracted and lost along the way. I see it all the time in the pro-ams that I play in each week. There are plenty of people with talent and experience that should do well but are suffering on the greens because they have no idea what to do, despite trying everything under the sun. Thankfully, James has kept me on the right path for nearly two decades. I know that if you have the correct information and approach to putting, you'll play better and enjoy the game more.

Because James knows what it's like to play for a paycheck and pay your bills with your performance, he's empathetic and "all in" for his students. He also has the unique gift of being able to understand the science and fundamentals without losing sense of the artistic part of being a great performer. Although he demands discipline from his students, he has a knack for boiling mechanics down to one or two simple keys, so you can free up your stroke and simply go "back and through." I've executed the same set of fundamentals to the best of my abilities since day one. Because of this,

Tom Pernice after sinking the winning putt at the 2014 Charles Schwab Cup Championship. Photo courtesy of PGA Tour.

and because I've been organized in my training and thoughts, I've had weeks where I putted as well as anyone on any tour in the world.

It doesn't surprise me that my partnership with James has stood the test of time. He's completely committed to being part of the solution for me. I'm confident that you'll get a lot out of this book, and I'm even more sure that you'll improve your game. Good luck, and enjoy the process!

TOM PERNICE, JR.
Murrieta, California
April 17, 2015

Prologue

Soon after I agreed to write *Your Putting Solution*, I shared the news with PGA Tour player Cameron Tringale, whom I've taught since 2012. Cameron's response wasn't what I expected—he laughed. "James," he said, "how are *you* going to fill up an entire book on putting? You always make it out to be so simple!" Panic and doubt immediately struck. Cameron was right, but as I began to draft an outline and jot down topics to discuss, I realized there was more to my putting system than either Cameron or I had realized. In the end, it was harder to decide what to omit than what to publish.

Now that the book is complete, I view Cameron's gut-check reaction as a compliment. I'm proud that my approach is considered "simple." As a coach and former playing professional, I know that simple is better when you're on the greens. Simplicity breeds clarity, and clarity fuels confidence. I could easily unleash a trove of knowledge and opinions on almost every topic that affects putting, but my job is to make you a great putter, not a great putting coach. As the great Bobby Jones once said, "the less you have to think about, the better you'll play."

Every golfer is different and has a unique set of problems. I have no idea what your stroke looks like. I couldn't fathom a guess as to your weaknesses or miss tendencies. But good putting isn't always about great technique. It's more about developing a clear approach to getting better. I've organized this book to reflect these truths. As such, you'll quickly learn what's necessary for *you* to improve and grow in confidence on the greens. The plan? Refocus whatever putting concepts and misconceptions you have swirling in your brain into a simple, clear, effective, and easy-to-execute plan.

Welcome to *Your Putting Solution*.

What Comes First: A Study of Skill

When it comes down to it, the only thing
that matters is making putts.

....

Although performance often follows form, and I'm excited by the opportunity to share my knowledge about the fundamentals of putting with you, this is not your typical how-to book. At no point will I say, "Master this special technique and you'll putt your best forever." To view putting from this perspective is a mistake that ultimately leads to inconsistency and frustration. Instead, think of *Your Putting Solution* as a "Can-You?" book. Can you do the things that are necessary to excel on the greens? And if not, what can you do to change your fortune? These are questions of skill, not technique, and that's something that I failed to understand during my playing days. Nor did I fully grasp it in the first decade of my teaching career. I get it now, and this knowledge has made me a more effective coach while simplifying the learning process for my students. The moment you embrace putting as a set of "skills" instead of hardset mechanics is the moment you open the door to long-term growth.

STEVE STRICKER'S "UGLY" STROKE

The following story should help prove my point. It was December of 2010, and I was sitting in the back row at a Titleist Performance Institute (T.P.I.) Level 3 Golf Professional Certification class in Orlando, Florida, listening to my good friend and T.P.I. co-founder Greg Rose lecture on the particulars of putting. (I was scheduled to share my opinions on wedge play following Greg.) About halfway through his talk, a hand shot up from the middle of the audience. With a heavy German accent, the person who raised his hand asked Greg to share his thoughts on the ideal putting-stroke shape. Specifically, he wanted to know if the correct path was one in which the putterhead traveled on an extension of the target line with the face remaining square from start to finish, or one that swung back and through on a slight arc, or one that followed the shaft plane with the face rotating noticeably open and closed.

Greg answered, "It doesn't matter. It's not about that." This wasn't the answer the man wanted or expected, so he pressed on. "No," he said, "one of those strokes has to be the best, which means the others must be wrong." Greg paused; I'm sure he was trying to think of the best way to get out of this mess. But then, instead of answering the question directly, he looked for me at the back of the room. "Hey, Sieck!" he asked. "Do you still have that video of Steve Stricker's stroke on your computer?"

Up to the podium I went, laptop in hand, unexpectedly thrust into the spotlight to make Greg's point for the group. I knew exactly what to say.

We all experience moments in life when we learn something new that profoundly affects our future, alters our perspective, and changes the way we think, plan, and react in everyday life. One of those moments happened for me on a warm Tuesday afternoon at the 2010 John Deere Classic in Moline, Illinois, six months before I took the stage in Orlando.

I had an appointment to meet one of my players on the TPC Deere Run practice putting green. As is the case with most professionals, he was running on "Tour-player time" (i.e., "I'll get there when I get there"). As I waited, I started to watch some of the other players work on their putting and noticed Steve Stricker on the far end of the green. Stricker is known as one of the best putters on the planet, so this was a prime opportunity to sneak in a little video and perhaps learn something from his genius. I focused my camera and recorded Stricker working his way around a hole, looking silky smooth as he rolled in a succession of eight-footers. I could have watched and recorded all day, but after a few minutes, my player showed up. I refocused my camera on my student and went to work.

That night in my hotel room, I downloaded the video into my coaching software program and replayed the Stricker frames. I couldn't believe my eyes. This was one of the best putters of all time?

Close-up video of Steve Stricker's putting stroke at the 2010 John Deere Classic.

Frame 1: Address. **Frame 2:** End of backstroke. **Frame 3:** Impact. **Frame 4:** Finish.

The images above are pulled straight from the Stricker video. As you can see in Frame 1 (address), the putterhead is sitting toe down and the ball is aligned not with the sweet spot but toward the heel. Moreover, the putterhead is aimed (dotted line) well to the right of his intended target. His backstroke is perfect as the putterhead swings back in a beautiful little arc (Frame 2), but his forward-stroke travels inside, or to the left, of his backstroke path. But wait, it gets worse. At impact (Frame 3), the putterface is about 6 degrees closed compared to its position at setup, and he strikes the ball slightly off the toe. The off-center hit causes the ball to start a fraction to the right of where the putterface is pointing at impact (solid line) but considerably left of his original aim. My last thought before turning off the lights was, "Wow, that's a shockingly awful stroke!"

I left the tournament the next morning to finish out the week teaching at my academy at Shadow Ridge Country Club back in Omaha. Following my Sunday lessons, I tuned into the John Deere telecast and watched slack-jawed as Stricker holed everything in sight. He finished at 26-under and won the tournament by four strokes. My body may have been relaxed as I lay sprawled out on the couch, but my mind was doing somersaults. A sickening thought struck me: "If I was Steve Stricker's coach, I would have made him so uncomfortable making his stroke "look" pretty (correcting his fundamentals) that he not only wouldn't have won the tournament, he probably would have missed the cut." As I pondered the meaning of this uncomfortable reality, a new belief cemented itself in my mind: Technique doesn't come first, performance does, and it doesn't necessarily matter what you do to perform. What's important is that you can.

STATING THE NEW OBVIOUS

I relayed this story to the T.P.I. certification class, and as I closed my laptop, I stated what the Stricker video experience had taught me:

1. Being able to repeat your stroke so that it produces predictable results is more important than attaining perfect technique.
2. Performance is dependent on a melding of essential skills that may or may not be influenced by mechanics.

The 100-plus instructors in attendance must have either been lost in thought or in shock, because I didn't get a single follow-up comment, not even from the inquisitive German. Hopefully, they got my point: It doesn't matter what stroke shape you choose, as long as you can define it, understand it, and master it. I'm sure many of the engineers or type A personalities reading this book are uncomfortable with this conclusion, but it's true, and to have a healthy relationship with your putter going forward, you must look at putting performance from this perspective.

THE ESSENTIAL SKILLS OF PUTTING

If you study the great putters throughout history—including champions such as Billy Casper, Jack Nicklaus, Brad Faxon, and yes, Steve Stricker—you won't find much in common from a technical standpoint. I'm sure that if I got them all on a SAM PuttLab I'd find several measurable "mechanical flaws" in each of their strokes. But so what? They owned what they did and possessed the ability to repeat it.

While mechanics may differ, there are a few things that all great putters do extremely well:

1. They start the ball on their intended line.
2. They see or feel the correct line to the hole.
3. They match that line with perfect speed.
4. They believe the ball is destined to end up in the hole.

In other words, great putters have *repeatable mechanics*, they start the ball *on line*, they *read greens effectively*, they roll the ball with *touch*, and they *ooze confidence*—the so-called "It" factor. These are the essential skills of putting. If you assume that Steve Stricker at the John Deere Classic was consistently starting the ball on the line he visualized (which he was), why would the particulars of the stroke itself matter? It's safe to say that Stricker can check off each of the above boxes; therefore, what I originally thought was an ugly stroke is actually a thing of pure beauty.

It's important for all players to understand that improving technique and becoming more skillful aren't necessarily the same things. Technical improvement often starts with an epiphany, while skill development is a process—an accumulation of experiences both successful and unsuccessful. Like bricks in a wall, the knowledge gained from achieving and failing stack on top of each other, creating something solid and strong. The natural state of technical execution is chaos, because we often change unwittingly. In contrast, once we develop a skill, it often endures.

It's the same as learning how to ride a bike. You start with some basic instruction—keep your feet on the pedals and push down to generate power—and learn that by gently turning the handlebar you can change directions. Gaining an understanding of these basic techniques gives you the confidence to climb on and begin making mistakes. The combination of falling down and having some success guides future actions, ultimately

The best lesson I learned as a putting coach was that performance comes first. So when I had the opportunity to work with all-time putting great Brad Faxon starting in early 2010, we skipped any discussion of technique and chose to work on the skill of matching line with speed.

increasing your *skill* as a bike rider. Eventually, you start showing off, popping wheelies and riding without holding on to the handlebar.

Does this mean that fundamentals don't matter? Not at all. Most players' fundamental flaws diminish the precision and consistency of execution, and small technical improvements often create huge jumps in performance. The players I coach work extremely hard on the fundamental techniques I lay out for them. Longtime client Charlie Wi works tirelessly on mastering his technical keys. In 2010, he led the PGA Tour in Total Putting. That isn't a coincidence. Now, don't take this as a license to shirk work if you're already a very good or even great putter. There are countless ways to refine and build skill. The key point is that when you practice putting, always prioritize skill development over some concept of "ideal." More important, when you make changes in your method, do so with the precise knowledge of how and why it will affect the essential skills listed above. Technique is a means to an end, not the end itself. Skill is the end game.

We'll explore the four essential skills in great detail throughout this book, beginning with Chapter 3. But first things first: Let's see what kind of putter you are. Better yet, let's assess your *skills* and see what you need to do to improve. Your putting lesson starts now.

How to Assess Putting Skill and Avoid the Pitfalls That Thwart Improvement

There are inherent problems associated with learning
how to putt, and because most players don't know
how to manage them, many of them are
getting worse at putting, not better.

I f you're one of the countless talented and hardworking golfers who, despite honest effort, putt worse now than you did a few years ago, take heart—this book is the solution. Trust me, I know why your practice time and experiences are causing poor performance on the greens. I suffered the same aggravation as a professional player, and I see it every week in my clinics and schools.

The biggest roadblock you're facing is that you don't know how to effectively train to improve your skills. When I'm working with one of my Tour students, we spend most of our time on skill training. If this is a priority for someone whose living depends on making putts, it should be for you, too.

The second mistake is that you tend to go it alone. Tell the truth: When was the last time you took a putting lesson from a qualified instructor? (Your buddy who three-putts every other green doesn't count.) Self-coaching on the greens is a confusing business. For instance, when you miss a makeable putt, you often don't know why, even if you make your best educated guess. This is a critical problem in the quest for long-term growth, because science tells us that learning is next to impossible without factual information about the result of an action. You can miss a putt a dozen different ways—you can choose the wrong line, aim poorly, commit an error in your stroke that creates off-center contact, apply too much or too little force, or use any combination of the above. It's also possible to miss putts by misjudging the slope, grain, or speed of the green, or even the wind. And even if you do get everything right, an imperfection in the green can cause the ball to do something that's impossible to predict. Try to find "factual information" in all that! Compounding the situation is the fact that you can miss a putt for one reason on one hole but for a completely different reason on the next.

Daunting, huh? This is the reality we all face, and because most of us don't have a clear way to assess our current skill set or own a mature enough approach to solve the riddle of how to improve, we make the ultimate fatal flaw: we tinker. We swap guesswork for logic, experiment on hunches, and when things don't go our way, we immediately try something new. After countless changes and trials that don't work, we find ourselves completely lost, unsure of anything despite years of experience. At this point, you are officially "getting in your own way."

This player shows up at my academy door with three putters in his bag, a fistful of frayed nerves, and a prescription for anxiety meds. There's a better way, and that's to develop a plan that embraces the specific intent for each step in the improvement process while providing confirmation that you're on the right track every time you practice. This eliminates the desire to guess and tinker. It's also essential that your approach is mature enough to set aside mechanics at the appropriate time and instead focus on skill development. Moreover, your plan must be simple to understand and simple to follow, yet effective.

This is the goal of *Your Putting Solution*: To formulate a plan that guarantees success, not one that hopes for it.

GETTING STARTED

Stop thinking of putting as a thing unto itself. There are too many parts and variables that must interrelate to produce desirable results. The correct approach is to think of putting in terms of the four essential skills I outlined above: starting the ball on your intended line, seeing or feeling the correct line to the hole, matching that line with perfect speed, and believing that the ball is destined to end up in the hole.

When you do this, you can more readily assess your proficiency in each. Only after you have factual information about your limitations or tendencies can you manage them and dive into the techniques and training that will improve performance within that area. As you improve each skill (independently of the others), the overall product (i.e., your ability to hole putts) improves along with it. In addition, you must avoid the common pitfalls to growth by understanding and believing in your method, as well as by committing to the keys of effective training. It takes discipline. Sustained improvement on the greens is the result of doing the right things the right way every time the putter comes out of your bag.

Step 1: Start a Journal

If you read my first book, *Your Short Game Solution*, you know that I'm a big fan of journaling and writing out a detailed training strategy. The act of writing or verbalizing specific intent aids both your commitment and accountability to the plan going forward. Start your putting journal (any blank notebook will do) by writing down a long-term attainable goal on the first page—a true vision about the new and improved putter you're destined to become. Make it something like, "I will execute on the greens confidently and reduce my stroke average by three shots per round within one year," or whatever you deem appropriate as long as it is both aspiring and measurable. Next, separate your journal into four sections with the following labels: (1) Assessments, (2) Technical Plan, (3) Training Plan, and (4) Personal Growth. Throughout this book you'll be asked to perform regular testing and record the results, as well as write down technical keys, training structures, performance notes, changes you make over time, and the little nuggets you learn on your journey.

Step 2: Assess Your Skills

The second step in creating your plan is to assess the particulars of your current skill set by performing the following three tests. In the 30 to 40 minutes it takes to complete them, you'll discover where you stand in relation to each of the four essential skills and thus what you need to manage and prioritize as you proceed with your plan.

Assessment No. 1: Starting the Ball on Line

Assessing your ability to start the ball on your intended line is an obvious place to begin your improvement journey, because if you can get the ball rolling in the direction you want it to go and swing your putter with confidence, you'll at least make more than your fair share of short putts. This is a big deal when it comes to scoring, because sinking the short ones takes pressure off both your finesse-wedge game and your lag putting. If you prove to be adept at this skill, you can then move on to assessing and improving the other three skills. If you fail the assessment, take a step back to focus on and train the individual variables and fundamentals that affect your ability to start the ball on the correct line (which we will cover in Chapters 3–5). Once you've mastered this skill, you can move on to the next one with confidence.

To be considered proficient at starting the ball on line, you must prove your ability to do it in all putting conditions: downhill, uphill, sidehill, and straight, because you'll face them all multiple times during the course of normal play. Any improvement process begins with establishing a baseline. Let's find yours.

25-Ball Dime Test

Place a dime on a gentle slope on the practice putting green (you won't need a hole for this assessment). Find the straight putt to the dime and drop five balls in the same spot on the green two feet from the coin. Your goal? Roll all five balls straight over the dime and stop them about four feet beyond it (for a total putt length of six feet). Listen for the "click" of the ball rolling over the dime on each attempt. Keep track of your hits and misses and record them in your journal in the assessments section under the heading "Straight Short Putt."

Repeat the test from the same location, but this time roll the balls over the dime to a spot about 13 feet beyond the coin (for a total putt length of 15 feet). Record the results under "Straight Medium-Length Putt" in your journal. Next, pick a spot on the green relative to the dime that would represent a right-to-left putt, and again roll the balls over the coin. Stop these putts about eight feet beyond the dime. Record your results under "Right-to-Left Putt," then repeat for a left-to-righter. Important: When performing the right-to-left and left-to-right assessments, don't putt from such a severe slope that a ball putted at the ideal speed breaks off before it reaches the dime. If the slope is relatively gentle (a 1 to 2 percent grade), it shouldn't move much during the first two feet of its roll.

Finish your assessment by rolling five balls over the dime on a short downhiller. You've now hit twenty-five putts (five putts from five different locations). Your results should tell you everything you need to know about your ability to consistently start the ball on line and help you decipher an appropriate solution.

Assess your ability to start the ball on line by putting over a dime on a short straight putt, medium-length straight putt, medium-length putts that break in both directions, and on a short, straight downhiller. If you can't hit the dime (set two feet in front of the ball) at least 80 percent of the time from each putt location, your setup and stroke fundamentals are holding you back from performing on the greens.

If you were able to hit the coin at least four times from every location (twenty total "hits"), that's good enough to be the best putter at your club and even outperform some of the Tour players I coach. In this case, treat yourself like I treat Brad Faxon—leave well enough alone and focus on improving the other three skills. Remember, you need to be proficient at all of them to perform well. If you didn't consistently hit the dime from all five positions, you need to find out why by diving into the fundamentals that affect this skill (Chapters 3 and 4). Ultimately, your belief in and execution of proper fundamentals will allow you to pass any reassessment with regularity.

Note: There's some simple math to the 25-Ball Dime Test. Given a perfectly flat putting surface, a perfect read, and appropriate speed, a ball that's struck so that it rolls over a dime set two feet in front of it on a direct line to the center of the cup is hit straight enough to find the hole from as much as 12 feet away. When you consider that your average Tour player sinks approximately 28 percent of their putts from this distance, it's safe to assume that starting the ball on line to this standard 80 percent of the time is more than good enough for you to dominate on the greens. If you passed the 25-Ball Dime Test but still aren't making putts, then one of the other essential skills are to blame, not this one.

DIME DIAMETER = 0.706"

10 FEET

2 FEET

HOLE DIAMETER = 4.25"

If you can roll the ball over a dime placed two feet in front of the ball on your starting line, your stroke is accurate enough to hit the hole from as far as 12 feet away on a flat green.

Assessment No. 2: Predicting the Correct Start Line

Green-reading is something that most players are notoriously bad at, even though they may tell you otherwise. It's a convoluted topic further complicated by the fact that, for most players, there are two reads for every putt: 1) the line they pick consciously and 2) their subconscious read or feel for aim and line once they settle over the ball. As you can guess, these reads often conflict. Completing the following test will help you decipher your overall green-reading skill, tendencies, and which type of read works best for you.

10-Ball Green-Reading Test

To assess your green-reading skill, you're going to hit five putts from both five and twelve feet. Explaining how to perform this assessment might take longer than it will for you to complete it, so hang in there and reread these instructions if you have to. On the practice green, find a slope with medium break (1 to 2 percent grade) and spread out five balls in a circle, each five feet from the cup. This will give you the variety of putts that you'll face in everyday rounds: uphill, downhill, right-to-left and left-to-right. Your goal is to judge the line and putt all five balls with a speed that allows them to travel a foot past the hole in the event they miss. On each putt, run through your normal green-reading process and record your conscious, or stated, read for the perfect start line for each putt at the intended speed. Copy the table below and record your reads in the appropriate row. Title it "Green-Reading: Short Putts." It should look something like this:

| | PUTT NUMBER | | | | |
	1	2	3	4	5
Conscious Read	Left edge	2" outside left edge	Straight	1" outside right edge	Right center
Subconscious Read					
Dime Hit?					
Putt Result					

Sample 10-Ball Green-Reading Test journal entry. Mark your initial read in the first row for each putt. You'll create charts for both five- and 12-foot putts.

Don't putt yet! The next step is to place a dime on your stated starting line about two feet in front of the ball, and push it down firmly into the green, just below the level of the putting surface, so it won't deflect the ball off line. For example, if your stated read for the first putt was "left edge," place the dime on a line that runs from the ball to the left edge of the hole. Repeat the process for the remaining putts from five feet.

Next, address each ball in succession as though you're going to putt it (but don't). Does the change in perspective (from read position to address position) make the dime appear as though it's on your stated line, or does your subconscious want you to aim above or below it? Note any "disagreement" in the second row of your green-reading assessment table, in-

Mark your initial read on each five-foot putt with a coin (highlighted by the small circles), then look for any discrepancies between your first read and what your eyes and feet tell you as you stand over each ball at address. Any disagreement between your conscious (first) and subconscious (address position) reads creates conflict and impairs your ability to start the ball on line.

dicating what your subconscious wants you to do, whether it's to play the intended break, play more break, or play less break (it'll probably be more).

Finally, it's time to stroke all five putts and fill out the last two lines of your assessment table. For each putt, note if the ball hit the dime on its way to the hole and record the result (make, miss on the low side, or miss on the high side). Although this test is more pragmatic than scientific, you can draw some basic—yet powerful—conclusions from the results.

If you rolled your ball over the coin, but the ball missed the hole (assuming reasonable speed), then you know that you misread the putt in the direction of the miss. Make a note of where the dime should have been placed. Is this more break or less?

If you miss the coin and the hole in the same direction, your read was probably fine, but your stroke was poor.

If you miss the coin, but the ball goes in the hole, you'll not only learn what your read should have been, but that you read greens much better subconsciously than consciously, which is critical information for improving your green-reading skills (Chapter 6). Record where the dime *should have* been placed (more break or less). Nailing your tendencies will help you better manage them going forward.

After you roll five balls from each starting position around the hole from five feet, move to a different hole and repeat the assessment from 12 feet. Again, record your results in a table. Title it "Green-Reading: Medium-Length Putts."

If you're a highly skilled green-reader who can also start the ball on line (i.e., over the dime), your tables should show agreement between your actual and subconscious reads, and that a majority or your putts rolled over the dime *and* went in the hole. Examine your recorded results critically and look for patterns. My guess is that most of you drastically under-read putts consciously, and then allow your subconscious to both misalign and pull or push the putt to get the ball somewhere near the correct line. A player of Steve Stricker's or Brad Faxon's caliber can probably hit all five coins and make all five putts from five feet, and hit the line at least four times in the 12-foot assessment with a couple of makes. And if they recorded their results in a table, they'd find very little internal conflict between where they decided to start the ball and their feel for the line as they addressed each putt.

Note: If your results tell you that you didn't set the coin in the correct

	PUTT NUMBER				
	1	**2**	**3**	**4**	**5**
Conscious Read	Left edge	2" outside left edge	Left center	1" outside right edge	Right center
Subconscious Read	Left edge	A cup out	Left edge	Right center	Right edge
Dime Hit?	Yes	No (left)	No (left)	Yes	Yes
Putt Result	Make	Make	Make	Low miss	Low miss

A properly completed assessment table provides useful clues about your green-reading strengths and weaknesses. Look for discrepancies between your conscious and subconscious reads, and note which one allows you to hit the dime—and sink putts—most often. In this example, the player would be much better off listening to his inner voice, because every time he sensed a different break standing over the ball, he was closer to reading the true line to the putt.

place on at least seven of the ten trials, then you need to study the physics of how slope and green speed affects putts and develop a better process for visualizing roll. (More on this in Chapter 6.)

Putting Without Conflict

Have you ever stepped into a putt knowing with 100 percent certainty that it was going to go in? It's an amazing feeling that every player experiences at one point or another. Call it the "Zone," a "Higher Power," or whatever you want, but I see it as the rare alignment of three important factors. First, your conscious read is factually correct, and you can visualize every part of the putt clearly. Second, your subconscious feel for the putt as you settle into the ball is in complete agreement with your conscious read. Third, you're so confident in the visual picture that you act without any sense of self-awareness, reacting only to the external cues without interference or clutter. That's why performing the 10-Ball Green-Reading Test is so important. The more you do it, and the more you improve your green-reading skills, the more likely your conscious and subconscious reads will match up. *Boom, baby!*

Assessment No. 3: Putting Touch

Your ability to avoid three-putting from long distance and drain those difference-making medium-length putts between eight and 15 feet is largely dependent on your touch. Touch is the ability to sense all of the factors that influence how the ball is going to roll on the green, and to expertly impart the correct energy to the ball so that it rolls up to the target with the anticipated pace. To test your current proficiency at distance control, perform the following two-part assessment.

Long-Lag Test

With three balls in hand, step off uphill 30-, 40-, and 50-foot putts to the same cup. Set a ball on the green at each distance, and starting with the 30-footer, lag each ball up to the hole. Score your results as follows: five points for a make, three points for a ball that comes to rest within three feet of the cup, one point for a ball that comes to rest within four feet of the cup, and zero for everything else. Add up your points, then repeat for 30-, 40-, and 50-foot

Test your ability to lag putts from 30, 40, and 50 feet. If your three-ball total using the scoring system above is less than 18, your touch is failing you on the greens.

downhill putts, as well as sidehill putts (either left-to-right or right-to-left) from the same three distances. If your cumulative score for all nine putts is 18 points or less, your ability to control distance—that is, your touch—is deficient and probably costing you several strokes per round. Improving your touch will definitely move you closer to meeting your desired goal.

Two-Hole Knockout Test

This test will assess your ability to control speed to the standard needed to make putts between eight and 20 feet with some regularity (those in the

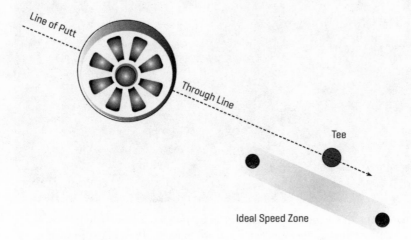

Two-Hole Knockout Test setup.

winner's circle are certainly "having their week" in this regard). Lay three balls down 10 feet from a cup and stick a tee in the ground one foot beyond the hole on the "through line" of your intended putt. Next, place a coin four inches beyond the tee on your through line (I prefer to put them off to the low side), and a second coin four inches in front of the tee.

Your goal with this drill is to roll all three balls either into the hole or into the eight-inch-long "ideal speed zone" bookended by the two coins. If you can't get all three balls to finish in the speed zone (or in the hole), pick them up and keep putting. Count the number of attempts it takes you to roll a total of three balls into the zone or the hole—in other words, to "knock out" that distance. That's your 10-foot score. Repeat the test on a completely different putt from 15 feet. If it takes you more than nine balls to knock out both holes, your sense of touch and ability to control distance

Two-Hole Knockout Test in action. The better you are at rolling the ball at the correct speed, the more likely you are to match the line to the speed, and to hole putts.

is in need of serious work. Note your score and your tendencies in your journal, and commit to improving your touch fundamentals using the training methods discussed in Chapter 7.

Assessment No. 4: "It" Factor

The last entry in my list of essential putting skills is mental prowess, or "it" factor, which allows you to execute with confidence. There's no assessment here, because growth in this area is something you should invest in daily, regardless of your current ability. Honestly, it's the master skill. Lacking belief in your abilities affects all putts, but it typically inflicts the most damage on the short putts you're supposed to make or during big moments, like when you need a putt to win your club championship or post your best score ever. Anyone who suffers from putting anxiety can tell you how difficult it is to perform on the greens when all you can think about is your next miss. In Chapter 8, we'll dive into the key elements of mental performance and embed proven strategies into your training regimen and process. As is the case with other putting skills, the more you improve your mental prowess, the more putts you'll actually hole.

NEXT STEPS

The assessments presented on these pages are powerful guides for customizing and fine-tuning your improvement plan. If you nailed one of the assessments, focus on the other three, consulting the appropriate chapters. If by some miracle you passed all of the assessments and still aren't making putts, then it's time to address the only possible area holding you back: the effectiveness of your training (Chapter 9). My guess is that you'll fail all three (I set high standards, and I hope you do, too), prompting you to begin your journey to better putting on the very next page by learning the foundational keys to starting the ball on line.

Skill 1:
Starting the Ball On Line
(Pre-Stroke Foundations)

The first step in learning how to roll putts in the direction
you intend is to clearly define how you plan on doing it,
leaving no variable or nuance unexplored. Your
competency depends on understanding and believing
in your method, coupled with effective training.

. . . .

If you were to paint a picture of your putting stroke, what would it look
like? If the image isn't clear and precise, or if it takes you a while to con-
jure it, you have a problem. How can you master something if you haven't
defined it? How can you commit to a plan that even you—its creator—
don't fully understand? You can't. Believing in and trusting your method
is an act of will, not a feeling you get after a few made putts. In other
words, if you don't own it, you'll never have it.

When the time is right to begin teaching a student technique, my first
task is not only to present a clear picture of how the putter should move
(based on his or her style), but to also make them understand the benefits
of moving it that way, as well as the fundamentals required to get it done.
The "doing" part of putting is the easy part. Let's face it—you don't have
to be a world-class athlete to stroke putts. As you'll learn, the quality and
consistency of your stroke depends more on your ability to grasp *why* you

swing the putter a certain way—and creating a feel for this movement—than it does your physical talents.

So let's get started. Lesson one: To consistently start the ball on line, you must:

1. Square the putterface to your intended line at impact
2. Contact the ball on the sweet spot of the putterface
3. Maintain a "neutral" putter path through impact
4. Strike the ball in the putter's center of mass

These are the building blocks of a successful stroke. Some are more critical than others, but all affect the start line in some way. As you begin the process, keep in mind that your stroke is a means to an end, not the end itself.

SQUARE PUTTERFACE

Contacting the ball so that it rolls in the direction you intend is mostly influenced by the angle of the putterface at impact. If your putter is pointing

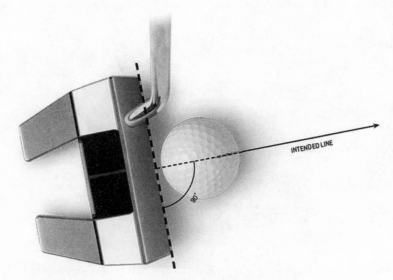

INTENDED LINE

When it comes to starting the ball on line, nothing is more important than squaring the face at impact. Face angle is king.

to the right of your intended line as you make contact with the ball, the putt will almost assuredly start to the right of your line, regardless of the other variables. The same goes if the putterface is pointing to the left at impact. Numerous studies indicate that face angle determines up to 85 percent of start direction. This isn't "coach-speak"—it's an absolute.

Therefore, the first step in starting the ball on line is to visualize what a properly aimed putterface looks like at address and then figure out how to re-create the same face angle at impact.

SWEET-SPOT CONTACT

Step two is to contact the ball on the sweet spot. Errors here don't affect start line as heavily as face angle, but they should definitely be avoided. If you make contact with the ball out toward the toe of the putterhead, it's highly likely the ball will start slightly to the right of your intended line and end up short of your target. Why? Because every putter twists, or rotates, when contact is made outside of the sweet spot (named as such because it's the spot on the putterface that's most resistant to twisting). Toe contact forces the putterhead to rotate open, creating a face angle that

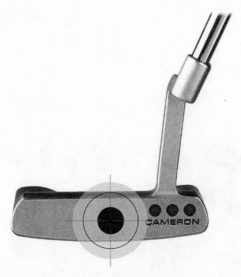

Putts struck on the sweet spot are more likely to start on line and with the correct speed. Missing the sweet spot causes the putter to twist, creating face-angle errors at impact as well as a loss of energy transferred to the ball.

points to the right of the intended line; the ball goes right and rolls with less energy. Impacting the ball with the heel area of the putterface does the opposite; the putterhead twists in the direction of the impact point and closes, resulting in a starting direction left of the intended line.

Until recently, the sweet spots of most mass-marketed putters were often mislabeled, because manufacturers tended to position contact marks and alignment aids in the horizontal center of the putterhead, not in the location of the club's maximum *moment of inertia* (the spot that offers the most resistance to twisting). Now, thankfully, manufacturers go through great pains to ensure that any putterhead markings coincide with the exact location of the sweet spot, so you can rest assured that if you strike the ball where you think the sweet spot resides, you'll be optimizing the stability of the putterface at impact. The research and development performed at outfits like Titleist's Scotty Cameron Studio are extremely advanced, using science to provide today's golfers with advantages other generations lacked.

STROKE PATH

Sweet spots are sweet spots, and any golfer can see the benefit of striking the ball with a square putterface. What's truly up for debate is the ideal putterhead path and stroke shape relative to the starting line. Path errors aren't as deadly as face errors, because the energy transfer and compression at impact with your putter (compared to the energy transfer and compression created when hitting a driver) is very low, providing some wiggle room for you to match the nuances of your body type, posture, and comfort level to your chosen path. The key, again, is to choose a particular shape, clearly define it, and then commit to it.

Unless there's strong disagreement, I try to get my players to swing the putter on a very slight, symmetrical arc—so slight, in fact, that the putter remains on (or nearly on) an extension of the target line with the face square to the line for two to three inches on either side of impact. An advantage to this stroke shape is that it doesn't require you to position the ball perfectly in the same place in your stance on every putt—you've got two or three inches on either side of the ball where the putter is moving straight down the line with the face square to the target. At any point in this zone, contact conditions fall within an acceptable standard, accommodating natural human error when it comes to positioning the ball in your stance.

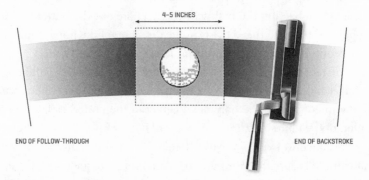

4–5 INCHES

END OF FOLLOW-THROUGH   END OF BACKSTROKE

Maintaining a neutral path four to six inches (two to three inches on each side of the ball) around the impact point helps you start the ball on line consistently and negates the need for precise placement of the ball.

What does this ideal stroke shape look like? Check out mine below. Although I don't practice much, I still manage to produce a fundamentally sound motion.

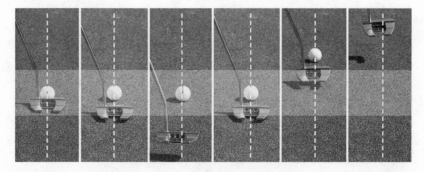

A great stroke shape runs down the target line through the impact zone and arcs symmetrically on the ends, with the face square to that arc at all times. The amount of arc may differ from player to player.

As you can see from these photos, my putterhead arcs slightly away from the target line (dotted) the farther it gets from its starting point. Also notice how square and straight everything is around the impact zone. Even though my stroke arcs, the face remains square to the arc from start to finish.

The exact amount of arc (and face rotation) you'll create in your stroke depends on your putting posture. In general, the more you bend from your

Your body type and the amount you bend over from your hips at address determine how much your putter will arc throughout the stroke. If you stand tall, your stroke shape will arc more than if you bend over.

hips at address (picture Michelle Wie), the less your stroke will arc, leading to less putterface rotation. Because I feel like less rotation and arc are beneficial for consistency, you'll notice that many of the players I coach on Tour bend over quite a bit from their hips at setup, with their weight evenly balanced over the arches of both feet.

BALL CONTACT POINT

The final part of your stroke picture is the putterface contacting the ball in the putterhead's center of mass, neither too high nor too low on the face. In order for this to happen, the putterhead should be ascending slightly (one to two degrees) into impact. The combination of these variables, along with the loft built into your putterface, will create optimal launch conditions, which are necessary to get the ball rolling on your intended line.

Launch conditions? Yes, putts do launch. On perfect impact, you create just enough upward movement to keep the ball from spinning either backward or forward for the first four to six inches of its roll. The angle of attack and resulting effective loft of the putter lift the ball a smidgen into the air (and out of any depression that the ball may have settled into) while pushing it toward the target parallel to the green's surface. Once the ball comes back into contact with the green, its forward momentum and lack of spin allow it to roll on your line without bouncing.

Optimal launch: A slight ascending strike is one factor that helps create the ideal effective loft at impact, which lifts the ball slightly off the ground with no spin for the first four to six inches of the putt.

Note: Grooves on a putter change this dynamic slightly—a ball hit with this type of putter will start rolling with topspin immediately after impact. Manufacturers who offer putters with grooved faces claim that this is beneficial, because a ball that immediately spins forward is less likely to be deflected off line by the ground. The testing I've seen on this matter has been far from scientific and at best has offered circumstantial evidence. Plus, it doesn't take into account different grass types and grass heights. Twenty years of coaching and a lifetime of putting experience make me a bit skeptical of these claims, to say the least.

Your Putting-Picture Recap
- Putterface aligned to your intended start line at both setup and impact.
- Putterhead path tracing a slightly symmetrical arc, with the putter-face remaining square to the arc throughout the stroke.
- Ball struck in the sweet spot of the putter, with the putterhead ascending slightly into impact.

NAILING THE FUNDAMENTALS

Now that the picture of your stroke and the key impact fundamentals are clear and complete, you need to come to terms with how you physically set up and execute your stroke to create the impact conditions that allow you to start the ball on your intended line without having to think about it. Although all fundamentals are interrelated to some degree, they're easier to understand and work on when you separate them into two distinct parts: those that happen pre-stroke, and those that occur during the stroke. For the remainder of this chapter, I'll focus on the pre-stroke fundamentals that fuel consistent impacts and accurate starting lines.

PRE-SWING FUNDAMENTALS THAT AFFECT YOUR ABILITY TO START THE BALL ON LINE

Body and club alignment at address both affect in-stroke motion and, therefore, stroke shape. I like my students to be comfortable; the more relaxed you are at address, the smoother your stroke will be and the easier it will be to repeat. So get cozy—just make sure your posture adheres to the following structure:

1. Set up so that the shaft of the putter is straight up and down, or perpendicular to the putting green, and your dominant eye is positioned two inches behind the ball (that is, away from the target). Most manufacturers build three to four degrees of loft into their putters

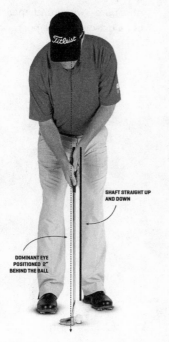

Critical pre-swing fundamentals from a face-on perspective.

SHAFT STRAIGHT UP AND DOWN

DOMINANT EYE POSITIONED 2" BEHIND THE BALL

because this creates an optimum amount of effective loft (static loft plus the strike angle of the putterhead) plus or minus shaft lean errors at impact. Manufacturers, however, assume that the user will set up with the shaft in a neutral position (straight up and down) at address and then return it to neutral at impact. If you feel more comfortable addressing the ball with your hands pressed forward or leaning back, you should have an equipment professional adjust the loft on your putter accordingly, so that you can maintain the ideal amount of effective loft.

2. Set up so your eyes are over an extension of the target line, or no more than one inch inside that line (in other words, no more than one inch closer to your body). This gives you the best vantage point to look down and see your intended line.

3. Set up so that the middle of your right hand sits directly under your right shoulder (or the shoulder on the same side of your body as the lowest hand on the grip). This will make it as easy as possible for you to swing the club on a neutral path.

4. Set up so that an imaginary line between your shoulders is parallel, or square, to your intended start line. This alignment will allow your hands to swing naturally along the target line. Notice that I said

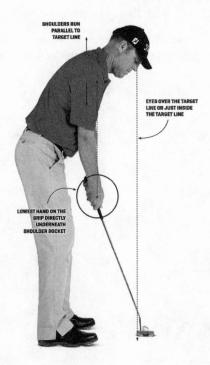

SHOULDERS RUN
PARALLEL TO
TARGET LINE

EYES OVER THE TARGET
LINE OR JUST INSIDE
THE TARGET LINE

LOWEST HAND ON THE
GRIP DIRECTLY
UNDERNEATH
SHOULDER SOCKET

Critical pre-swing fundamentals from a down-the-line perspective.

I wanted your shoulders square, but that I didn't say anything about your feet. That's often a matter of eye dominance and comfort. Generally, left-eye dominant players (right-eye dominant if you're a lefty) see the line better if they set up with a square stance and the ball slightly forward of center, so they can get their dominant eye just behind the ball. Right-eye dominant golfers (left-eye dominant if you're a lefty) tend to feel more comfortable with an open stance; this allows them to cock their head a little toward their trail shoulder and look down the line more easily with their dominant eye. The ideal ball position for this type of golfer is typically dead center.

MASTERING YOUR SETUP

These four setup fundamentals are simple to understand and require no real special ability to master, but how do you know if you're accurately executing them? Obviously, intent means nothing. There's a huge difference between what we feel and what's real. It can't be subjective or up for debate—you need to know with 100 percent certainty that you've got them down pat. My advice? Check your setup fundamentals using my Mirror-Setup Drill (explained below) at least once a week. It'll take no more than a minute, and you'll be using that time wisely.

Mirror Set-Up Drill

Step 1: Find a full-length mirror in your home and get into your address position with your body facing the mirror. From this vantage point, check that the shaft is sitting 90 degrees to the ground and that your dominant eye is approximately two inches behind the ball. Adjust both hand and upper-body positioning until you nail these important setup fundamentals.

Step 2: Rotate to your left a full 90 degrees so that you're setting up to putt away from the mirror. (If you putt left-hand low, set up as though you're putting into the mirror.) Check that your arms dangle freely from your shoulders and that the middle of your right hand sits directly below the center of your right shoulder. (If you putt left-hand low, make sure that the middle of your left hand sits directly below the center of your left shoulder.) If the image in the mirror doesn't reflect this, adjust your hip hinge or arm position until you get it right.

Work on your pre-stroke fundamentals using a mirror at least once a week. Even Tour players fall into bad habits. Keep them at bay with a quick and easy weekly checkup.

Step 3: Confirm that your shoulders look square to your intended line (when you look back into the mirror, your right shoulder should hide your left, and vice versa if you putt left-hand low). Adjust if necessary.

Step 4: Make sure the ball is under your eyes, or just outside them, and confirm that your putter is soled flat on the ground. If the heel is down and the toe is up, your putter is too upright for your posture and you'll need a fitting professional to adjust it for you. Obviously, the same can be said if your putter is too flat (toe down), or too long or too short. You're better off adjusting the fit of your putter to your most comfortable posture and the proper setup fundamentals than adjusting your setup to a putter that doesn't fit.

Now that you've attained a fundamentally sound setup, measure the distance from the ball to your toe line by marking an alignment stick or using the length of your putterhead to create a measurement. For example, when he's training, PGA Tour player Cameron Tringale puts a tee in the ground two and a half putterhead lengths from the inside of the ball to mark his toe line, or the distance he stands from the ball. Because he checks both this distance and his eye positions daily, his posture and body orientations never change—a key to mastery.

THE POWER OF STYLE CHOICES

Hopefully you realize that when it comes to the proper setup fundamentals, I'm not asking for much—you can nail them in a few minutes with the mirror drill. However, you may have address position questions I have yet to answer, such as "Which grip should I use?" or "How firmly should I

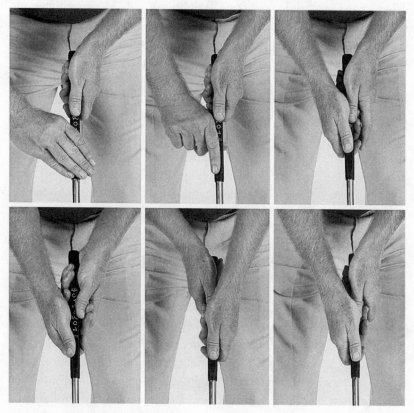

Style choices, like which grip you use, are not fundamentals—go with what gives you the most control.

grip the club?" I wouldn't think of trying to answer those, because there's a difference between fundamentals (things everyone should do) and style choices (things that *you* should do because they work for you). Make any style choices that suit you, just make sure that they help you achieve the body and club alignments discussed in this chapter. Your style choices will differ from mine and from most golfers you know. Tiger Woods uses his trail arm to dominate his stroke and grips the putter very lightly. His good friend, Steve Stricker, grips his putter with maximum pressure and swings it using his lead arm and hand. They're completely opposite styles, but they both allow the user to comfortably control the club and, more important, to repeat the motion. Whether you hold the club in your fingers or palms, have a fat grip or a skinny one, putt cross-handed, traditionally, or with the claw—it doesn't matter as long as those choices allow you to achieve the setup fundamentals we've discussed and give you a high measure of control over the club.

With these criteria in mind, think through the style choices you've already made and the ones you've been thinking about adopting and commit to those that feel best. I, for example, feel more in control of the club with a skinny grip running through my fingers, which is the opposite of the current trend on Tour. Champions Tour player Tom Pernice, Jr. switched to a left-hand low, or cross-handed, grip a decade ago after constantly struggling to get his shoulders square at address with a traditional hand placement. This change has made a huge difference in his comfort level and consistency. Your style choices are unique to you. Make them for the right reasons, and then commit to them.

GETTING POINTED IN THE RIGHT DIRECTION

The scary thing about putting is that establishing and perfecting great fundamentals means nothing if you can't aim. Starting the ball on line when the actual line is three degrees left won't save you any strokes. In fact, it'll drive you from the game. I offer three effective strategies in this regard. The first is to choose the right putter. Its design—head shape, hosel type, shaft offset, loft, alignment markings, etc.—has a tremendous effect on where your eyes tell you to aim the putter. If you have an aiming error tendency and a miss tendency in the same direction, finding a putter that you can aim is often the simplest and most effective fix.

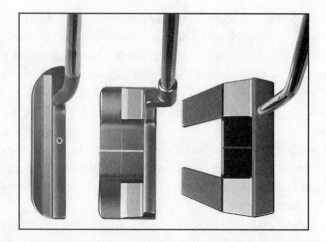

The best putter for you isn't the one that looks the sharpest or the model used by your favorite Tour player; it's the one designed to augment your in-stroke strengths and minimize your mistakes, including poor aim. If, for example, your putterface often rotates too much relative to the path, consider a face-balanced putter (far right). If the putterface either rotates closed in the backstroke or opens up in the through-stroke, a heel-shafted putter with more mass toward the toe (far left) may help you. Grip shape and size is an issue of comfort and control and needs to be worked through individually. As with any equipment choice, your best bet is to pay a visit to a trusted clubfitter.

FINDING THE PERFECT PUTTER

When choosing a putter, prioritize the following criteria in this order:

1. Your ability to aim it
2. Solidness of the hit
3. Proper length and lie angle for your setup fundamentals
4. Weight
5. Balancing (toward the toe, heel, or face)

Recently, an aspiring Tour professional called me in a panic because of his bad putting leading up to the second stage of PGA Tour Q-School. Even though he was missing all of his putts to the right, I knew that his stroke fundamentals were relatively sound, because he had sent me some video days earlier. So when I arranged to meet him at the tournament site, I told him to bring every good putter he owned. Sure enough, four of the five putters he brought, including the one he had been using leading up to the event, biased his aim well to the right. The one that didn't, ironically, was devoid of any alignment markings, the absence of which forced him to look at the face to aim instead of the line on the putterhead. By finding the right putter design, and making a slight change in his training to boost his confidence, he putted lights-out and made it through qualifying with flying colors.

When choosing a putter, forget about what it looks like. Can you aim it? Test different designs until you find one that fits your eye by setting up to a straight-in six-footer and asking a buddy to stand behind you and give you feedback on your aim.

The second strategy to improve aim is to actually practice it in a learning environment. Without intelligent practice, aiming errors can and will pop up, mostly as a response to poor stroke fundamentals. For example, if you have a stroke that consistently produces a left miss and you hit enough putts, you'll subconsciously develop a right-aim error. Your subconscious is taking care of you, so to speak, but it's a short short-term solution beset by long-term inconsistency. The good news is that you can effectively change the way you see targets and aim at them through proper training in as little as three weeks. You'll be doing this as part of *Your Putting Solution* training plan (Chapters 9–11), so where you currently stand with this ability is irrelevant. Once you get going with your putting workouts, you'll soon be aiming perfectly without any doubts.

Lastly, when all else fails, you can mark your ball with a line, stand behind it and use your binocular vision (in other words, while looking at it with both eyes—this is how we see in our day-to-day life) to align it toward your intended line, and then set the putterface perpendicular to the ball line. This eschews the traditional aiming process altogether, and has both its pros and cons. We'll get into this technique more thoroughly in Chapter 6 when we broach green-reading skills.

Skill 1:
Starting the Ball On Line
(In-Stroke Foundations)

The address-position fundamentals outlined in the previous
chapter are designed to put you in the best possible
position to start your putts on line. The ball, however,
can't start rolling by itself. That's determined by
how you generate the motion of your stroke.

Once your setup fundamentals are in order, the act of stroking the
ball on your intended line is nothing more than maintaining a suspension point and staying stable throughout your motion. See—I told you
it was going to be easy! But as with anything in this book, it's critical for
you to understand *why* I'm asking you to maintain a suspension point
(whatever that is) and remain stable. Coming to terms with these concepts
and what it feels like to execute them is critical to the improvement process and allows for the best possible results. Let's get started.

IN-STROKE FOUNDATION NO. 1:
MAINTAINING YOUR SUSPENSION POINT

A great putting stroke is similar to a pendulum in that it moves around a
fulcrum, or a fixed point. Your ability to establish and maintain the ful-

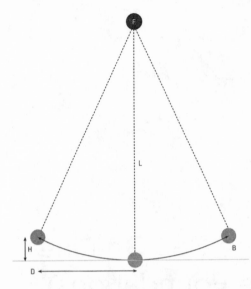

The rhythmic, consistent swing of a pendulum results from the establishment of a fixed suspension point, or fulcrum (F). In this diagram, H is the height of the swing (or stroke), D is the displacement (length of backstroke), B is the bob shape and mass (the putterhead) and L is the length of the pivot arm (arm hang plus shaft length).

crum, or suspension point, along your set up determines the shape of your stroke. Move the fulcrum and your stroke goes haywire.

It's easy to visualize the concept of a suspension point when a player is putting with a long or belly putter—the butt of the grip is touching the body, creating a fixed point about which the putter swings. Because the

Just like a swinging pendulum, your stroke must move back and through around a fixed point—a "virtual" suspension point that you establish at address and maintain throughout your stroke.

suspension point is physically fixed to the body with a belly or long putter, it's much easier to coordinate the movement of the different body parts involved with executing a proper stroke. No doubt, belly and long putters have helped a lot of players better control the forces applied to the club and sink more putts, but since the USGA has deemed this advantage illegal (Rule 14.1b, effective January 1, 2016), you must now come to terms with this principle and learn correct movement using a traditional-length putter (or a belly or long model that isn't fixed to your body).

With a short putter in your hands and both arms swinging freely, the pivot arm of the pendulum is not actually an extension of the club itself, but rather a vertical line connecting a point on your upper body to your hands. The suspension point of your pendulum is more of a "virtual" one. As such, it's trickier to control compared to putting with a belly or long putter. When assessing suspension point using video, I mark and extend the shaft upward with a vertical line in four separate frames: 1) setup position, 2) end of the backstroke, 3) impact, 4) the completion of the stroke. If the player I'm analyzing properly maintains his or her suspension point, each of these lines will meet at a fixed point somewhere near the golfer's sternum.

An imaginary line running up from the butt of the grip to your body should point at the same place on your sternum at address, at the end of the backstroke, at impact, and at the end of your forward-stroke. This ideal pendulum putting motion results from blending all of the moving parts in your stroke in a coordinated fashion.

Expert at Work! For additional clarification on the suspension-point fundamental, watch a special video detailing this concept at jsegolfacademy .com/index.php/james-suspension-point.

With a short putter, maintaining the suspension point of your pendulum stroke is easier to understand than execute, especially if you've never felt the correct motion. A lot of accepted wisdom on how to accomplish this fundamental does more harm than good. Contrary to popular opinion, it's not about "locking your elbows and wrists," "rocking your shoulders," "keeping your triangle," or any version of "not breaking down." Rather, maintaining your suspension point is achieved by coordinating and blending all the moving parts in your stroke and using them in the correct ratio to one another. (By moving parts, I mean everything above the belt save for the top of your spine, your head, and your eyes. More on that later in the chapter.) Put into even simpler terms, learning and mastering your suspension point is about being able to "feel" the correct motion on a consistent basis. Luckily, I have a magical drill to help you get it right.

How to Properly Maintain Your Suspension Point

Indoors, set up to an imaginary ball while facing a wall. Make sure you get into your address posture using the perfect body alignments described in the Mirror Setup Drill in Chapter 3. Next, shuffle your feet forward until the crown of your forehead rests gently against the wall. Once you're set, slowly inch the puttershaft up through your hands until the butt of the grip touches the center of your sternum (or slightly left of center if you're left-eye dominant or grip the putter left-hand low). Keep your arms hanging in the same position as you raise the shaft toward your body, so that the shaft remains perpendicular to the ground (resist the temptation to lift your hands outside your shoulders and get the putterhead under your eyes.) If you do it correctly, your hands will block your view of the putterhead.

With the butt of the club fixed in position, swing your hands, arms, and chest in unison back and forth, keeping your elbows soft and your grip pressure constant (photos, page 40). Swinging in this manner with your forehead against the wall will not only give you the feeling of disassociating your shoulder and chest movement from your spine (no side bend), but will also create the proper blend of movement between your wrists, elbows, arms, chest, and shoulders.

Take inventory of the sensations, because this drill gets every body segment moving in the correct sequence and with the correct speed and force relative to the others, allowing you to maintain the suspension point with very little effort.

Executing this key fundamental results in great stroke shape and control, setting you well on your way to consistently starting your putts on line. After you get a feel for the motion, soften your hold on the shaft so the grip falls down into your hands. With your forehead still resting against the wall, assume your normal setup and repeat the drill. Continue as necessary or until you can transfer the motion to real strokes on the practice putting green or out on the course.

SUSPENSION-POINT FAULTS AND FIXES

As a coach, I like to think positively, as in "If you just do the Suspension-Point Drill and forget everything else, you'll be fine." But I know that old tendencies die hard and can creep into your motion at any moment, despite your best intentions. Reviewing these "death moves" and the fixes that allow you to maintain your suspension point if and when they work their way back into your stroke can go a long way toward helping you execute on the greens.

Suspension-Point Drill

1. Get into your putting stance with your forehead resting against a wall.

2. "Shuttle" the grip up through your hands until the butt of the handle touches your sternum.

3. Make your backstroke keeping your forehead on the wall and your grip snug against your sternum.

4. Do the same thing on your forward-stroke. Note the feels that maintaining your suspension point creates.

Suspension-Point Error No. 1: Early Rotation (Block Finish)

NO!
Rotating your chest ahead of the swinging action of your arms and hands tends to open the face at impact.

What It Is: Your chest rotates faster than the speed of your arm swing in the transition from backstroke to forward-stroke.

What It Does: Creates a loop to the outside in your transition, an open putterface at impact, and weak pushes to the right of your intended line.

The Fix: Try My Trail-Arm-Only Drill.

Grip your putter using your right hand only. With your left hand, hold the clubhead of your longest iron. Settle into your putting address posture, and extend your left arm forward so that you can rest the grip of the iron on the ground just outside your intended line of putt. This will stabilize your chest and keep you from rotating too early and/or blocking your finish. Next, make as normal a putting stroke as possible using only your right arm, putting underneath the "bridge" created by your left arm and the iron (photos, page 42). The focus here is to sense how your right arm "closes"

Trail-Arm-Only Drill: Create a "gate" to putt through by holding an iron upside down with your left hand. Use your right hand to "putt past your center" without prematurely rotating your chest.

against your chest at the start of the forward-stroke, allowing the putterhead to release. This drill will teach you to "putt past your center," which all great putters do. Two of my PGA Tour students, Charley Hoffman and Tom Pernice, Jr., use a "back-and-through-past-my-head" mantra almost every week to manage this tendency and boost their performance on the greens.

Suspension-Point Error No. 2: Handle Carry

What It Is: Moving the handle of the club more than the putterhead during the takeaway, resulting in a backward-leaning shaft at impact.

What It Does: Launches the ball with too much backspin, which creates an unpredictable roll, a closed putterface at impact, and pulled putts.

The Fix: Try My Stacked-Quarter Drill.

I can't imagine worse advice than "take the putterhead back low and slow," yet you hear it on TV and read about it in books and magazines all

Stacked-Quarter Drill: Stack two quarters about four inches behind the ball on an extension of your target line. Your goal? Keep the stack intact as you swing back and through.

the time. Think about it: If your stroke is meant to copy the swing of a pendulum, it has to rise at the far ends of the arc (the "H" in the diagram on page 36). Why would you fight this natural arc by keeping the putterhead low to the ground? (For those of you keeping track at home, your stroke actually arcs in two directions: one relative to the target line and the other relative to the horizon.)

To ensure that you start your stroke properly, punch a small hole in the green using a tee and place your ball in the resulting depression. Grab two quarters and stack them on top of each other about four inches behind the ball on an extension of your target line. Rehearse the motions outlined in the Suspension-Point Drill. After a few strokes, drop the putter grip into your hands and make a stroke. If you maintain your suspension point and don't carry the handle, the putterhead will trace the correct vertical arc and just miss the stack of quarters both going back and coming through. (Make sure you're missing the quarters because you're swinging the putter on an arc and not simply lifting it off the ground.) The drill is complete after five successful strokes.

Suspension-Point Error No. 3: Trail-Hand Flip

What It Is: Your chest and left arm prematurely decelerate in the forward stroke while your right hand continues to apply force.

What It Does: Creates poor contact, makes distance control difficult, and produces putts that start to the left of the intended line.

The Fix: Try My Lead-Arm-Only Pause Drill.

Allowing your bottom hand (the right hand for most players using a traditional grip) to dominate your stroke is usually a result of poor rhythm, a premature deceleration of your chest and arms, and an unhealthy anticipation of impact. To rid yourself of this affliction, find a straight three-foot putt and lay an alignment stick on the green with the tip nearly touching the inside edge of the cup. Set up to the inside of the stick and set a ball on the opposite side of it so when it comes time, you can stroke the ball into the hole without any interference.

While holding your putter with your lead hand only, make five practice strokes just inside the stick, focusing on the spot on the ground where the ball would be. On each stroke, pause at the end of your motion. Note the distance that the toe of the putter has moved away from the

NO! Flipping the putterhead ahead of your hands through impact is a big-time putting no-no. The loss of suspension point resulting from this error closes the face. You'll pop the ball up, have difficulty controlling distance, and miss left most of the time.

alignment stick, as well as any face rotation. Because this is a three-footer and the swing is relatively small, the toe of the putter should remain close to the alignment stick from start to finish. (Remember, the putterhead travels on a *slight* arc, with the putterface remaining square to the arc throughout the motion.) If you make the mistake of allowing your bottom right hand to "flip," the face will look noticeably closed at the finish and the putterhead will be substantially inside the rod. Following these five practice strokes, make five more with both hands on the club and remember to check your finish. They should look identical to those made with just the lead hand on the club.

After completing these strokes, address the ball on the other side of the stick and make the putt. Once again you will be checking the finish while using the stick as a reference. The drill is completed after you make five three-footers with the correct clubhead orientation in the finish. Ten practice swings and five or so putts shouldn't take more than a few minutes, but give it full focus and pay attention to the details for maximum benefit.

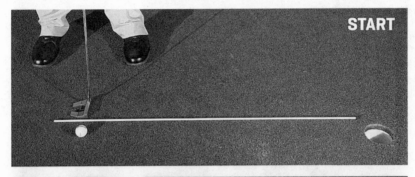

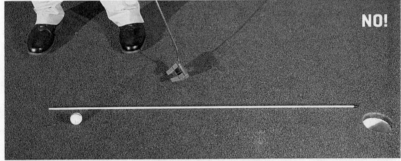

Lead-Arm-Only Pause Drill:

Part 1: Make practice strokes using an alignment stick as a guide. Check that the putterface hasn't over-rotated or swung too far to the inside at the finish. It will be difficult to consistently make short putts if it does.

Lead-Arm-Only Pause Drill:

Part 2: After assessing your finish position relative to the alignment stick on your practice strokes, putt for real.

Roll practice putts with your palms open and facing each other. This will teach you to maintain a constant grip pressure throughout your stroke and activate your "big" muscles to help you control the putterhead and maintain suspension point.

ONE MORE DRILL FOR GOOD MEASURE

Another great exercise that will solve practically any suspension-point error is the Prayer Drill. It's one of my favorites because it creates an awareness of the muscles you need to use in order to maintain your suspension point throughout the stroke—the key to swinging your putter like a pendulum.

To start, get into your normal address position, then open your hands and press your palms against the sides of the grip. Your palms should be directly facing each other, as though you're praying. Now make a few practice strokes, and then roll some putts for real. Because your hold on the putter has been weakened, you're forced to use the bigger muscles in your chest, shoulders, and core to move the putter, which allows you to keep your grip pressure constant throughout the stroke. If you can sink putts performing this drill, you're on the right track.

For those of you who prefer work with a training aid over a drill, I like one called True Pendulum Motion—TPM. It is a device that hooks onto your putter and is both easy to use and effective while creating the same sensations the Prayer Drill does.

IN-STROKE FOUNDATION NO. 2: STABILITY

The second in-swing fundamental that affects your ability to start the ball on line is stroke stability. For ultimate performance, you need to stabilize in two very different ways. The first is by engaging your core, a process that entails aligning your pelvis to your spine and holding everything in place as you putt. This is critical because it allows you to disassociate your upper and lower body, a necessary step for maintaining your suspension point. Any change in balance in any direction or lower-body rotation will wreak havoc on the shape of your stroke. As such, when you take your address, you must hinge at the hips and set your core in a manner that promotes stability.

In Chapter 3, I mentioned that your weight should be evenly balanced between the heels and balls of each foot. This is important, because if you set up with your weight too far back toward your heels, it's nearly impossible to get your hips and spine in a neutral alignment so you can properly engage your core. The telltale sign of this error is a rounded upper back at address, which inhibits arm swing and promotes recurring back pain during practice.

The simplest way for me to help you learn the feel for the correct balance and hip stability at address (which will carry forward into your stroke) is to create *instability* and then let your mind and body's natural inclination for balance take care of the rest. With that in mind, I created the following drill.

Worm Stability Drill

Step 1: Roll up a towel into a "worm" shape.

Step 2: Place the towel under the arches of both feet, then get into your address position and rock forward.

Step 3: Rock backward toward your heels.

Step 4: Settle your weight over your arches. Now you're balanced and stable.

Worm Stability Drill

Take a towel and turn it into a worm-like roll approximately two or three inches in diameter. (If the towel lacks the necessary thickness, you may have to fold it once before rolling it to get the proper size.) Once you've made your "worm," lay it on the putting green and grab your putter. Set up for a practice stroke while standing on the towel. Make sure the towel is directly under the arches of both feet. You're now unstable. Rock onto your toes and you'll immediately recognize that this position doesn't feel strong or athletic. Rock in the opposite direction, all the way back to your heels, and you'll experience even more instability. After a second, shift your balance to find the middle ground between your heels and toes, right over your arches, and then hold your pose. As your body fights for stability with that balance, it will automatically shift your pelvis to a position in which it aligns with your spine, and your core muscles will engage. This is the correct amount of hip hinge and posture for you. Finish the drill by making ten continuous strokes back and through to learn the true feel of disassociating your hips from your chest and shoulders.

Hip and spine muscular stability are important if you want to be able to perform your fundamentals with ease. The specific muscles groups called into question are the gluteals (maximus and medius), deep core stabilizers (multifidus and tranverse abdominals), and outer core muscles (rectus abdominis, quadratus lumborum, erector spinae, etc.) If you're going to leave no stone unturned on your way to putting greatness, then you should add a few simple exercises to your weekly routine to make it easy. The foremost expert in golf biomechanics, Dr. Greg Rose of the Titleist Performance Institute, shows you how in a special video. Watch the clip and get after it.

HOW TO STABILIZE YOUR STROKE WITH YOUR EYES

The second way to create in-stroke stability involves your eyes. How you use them before, during, and after your stroke is critical to performance on the greens. When most players think of vision's role in putting, the first thing that comes to mind is quality of perception. Am I 20/20? Can I perceive the nuances and cues provided by the green in order to read it correctly? For the first thirty-three years of my playing and coaching career

Expert at Work! Dr. Greg Rose of the Titleist Performance Institute explains how to strengthen and train the muscles responsible for in-stroke stability in this special video at jsegolfacademy.com/index.php/rose-stability.

this was my view, but now I know that it's more appropriate to think of vison in terms of how your eyes best communicate with your brain so that your muscles get the information they need to stroke the ball into the cup. There are tricks to it, and it's a topic I broach with every student, because it's often a clear line of demarcation between great and poor putters. Eye movements are both physical fundamentals and beacons of mental strength. And as proof that life is often stranger than fiction, I learned all this one sunny day on the way to the loo.

It was around 2000, and I was at Colonial Country Club in Fort Worth, Texas, for what was then the PGA Tour's MasterCard Colonial Tournament. My busiest day when I'm out on Tour is usually Tuesday, and I remember being out on the putting green with one of my clients, Skip Kendall, whom I started coaching in 1998. After finishing with Skip and before tracking down my next client, I walked into the player's locker room and was met with the most unexpected sight: In the hallway, just outside the bathroom, was a man sitting at a small desk housing a sizable computer and several strange-looking gadgets. Next to him was a Tour player stroking putts on the carpeted floor wearing a weird-looking helmet with wires connecting it to the equipment on the desk. Generally, I'm a "mind my own business" kind of guy, but this setup was too bizarre to ignore. I walked over to the line to eavesdrop.

Standing in front of me was PGA Tour player Loren Roberts, known as the "Boss of the Moss" for his legendary putting ability. Within minutes, a technician began applying sensors to various parts of Roberts's scalp, then handed him the helmet. It looked like something a Hells Angel would wear, except for two small cameras mounted on top (think GoPro) and two small mirrors on each side that protruded out like the eyes of an insect. When given the green light, Roberts addressed a ball and stroked it into a fake cup approximately ten feet away. As he putted, an electroencephalogram (EEG) recorded his brain's electrical activity on a scrolling piece of paper while the helmet cameras tracked and recorded his eye movements reflected in the mirrors. At the conclusion of the test, Roberts shed the helmet and wires and sauntered off. I was the only bystander left and since no one else was around, I did what anybody would do in that circumstance: I stepped in to take my turn.

On went the sensors and helmet. I addressed the ball and hit my best putt. As the gear was removed, I glanced down at my EEG graph. It looked like it had just recorded an earthquake, with wild spikes running up and down across the paper readout. What interested me was that my EEG was completely different than Roberts's. His readings were nearly flat, with just a few gentle waves. Not understanding the significance, I asked the man sitting at the desk what it all meant. He told me that when your eyes change focus from one object to another, when you blink, or when you take on a new thought, your brain generates neural electrical impulses that result in spikes in the EEG printout. An epiphany hit like a ton of bricks raining down from above: Great putters (and few are greater than Loren Roberts), putt with quiet eyes and a calm spirit, and despite 30-plus years of experience and immeasurable training, I had neither.

Ironically, I chose to study and dedicate my professional coaching life to the short game, largely because when I played in college and on the Asian and South American tours, my struggle with this aspect of the game kept me from fulfilling my dreams. Deep down, I craved answers to my short-game problems. My stroke looked good, but I often played without courage, and never putted to Tour standards. Unlike the Boss of the Moss, I had a "noisy" brain. Perhaps that's the real difference between those who are meant to play and those who are destined to coach: The former execute with internal coherence, the latter in complete chaos.

Honestly, I don't know the name of the organization responsible for the testing at Colonial. I never thought to ask, which seems a bit stupid now, but the only thing that mattered as I walked out of the locker room and back out onto the practice putting green was that there was a key attribute to putting that I knew nothing about. Once I returned home, I immediately sought out and read as much research as I could on vision and eye movement.

The most interesting thing I came across was a process called the "Quiet Eye" technique. The term was coined in 1996 by Dr. Joan Vickers, head of the Neuro-Motor Psychology Laboratory at the University of Calgary. Quiet Eye refers to the gaze behavior just before, during, and after movement in aiming tasks such as shooting a basketball or putting. Almost all elite putters have a high efficiency in their gaze pattern, or what scientists call "saccades." In an efficient saccade, the golfer scans toward the target, locates it, fixates, then turns back to the ball, settling his or her eyes at address for at least one second before starting the stroke. (In other sports such as tennis or basketball, a successful saccade lasts just fractions of a second—think Steph Curry hitting a fadeaway jumper. Most successful golfers are much more deliberate with their eye scans because they're afforded the luxury of time.) The communication flow from the eyes to the brain and muscles is subconscious and clear, creating zero doubt about the target's position in space as well as where the club is going to contact the ball.

Your eyes are the window of the soul—and the cup. Training methods such as the Quiet Eye technique not only help you get a better picture of the line and expected roll, but allow your innate athleticism to propel the ball down the starting line.

Once good putters settle their eyes, they react to the information sent to their brain. Their physical focus remains constant during the motion and for a count after. Poor putters, on the other hand, often have imprecise scan paths. Their gaze to the target is often too short in duration, inconsistent, and far too general. In addition, their physical focus often changes during their putting motion, usually moving toward their left foot as the putter nears impact. They're not sure where the target is in space, and the neural electrical pulses generated by the change in focus can create involuntary muscular contractions at precisely the wrong time.

The goal of the Quiet Eye technique is effective communication between your eyes and brain as they sense the target and the ball, as well as maintaining a quiet mind throughout your stroke. As such, I view the physical skills involved in utilizing the Quiet Eye technique to be synonymous with the mental attribute of having a "calm spirit," because if you're overly concerned or worried about a putt, it's very difficult to keep your gaze quiet during your motion. The eyes are the window of the soul; liars often look down and to the left just after lying, and highly trained poker players can detect stress in their opponents just by watching their eyes. Clearly, it takes a measure of trust to send the ball on its way without changing your focus to anticipate impact or the impending result. More on this in Chapter 8.

Note: At numerous times in this book, particularly when discussing eye movement, the physics of green-reading, and visual perception, I'll be offering an amateurish summation of research done by extremely smart and highly trained people. For a more accurate and complete view of this scholarship, I suggest you search out and read the works of Dr. Joan Vickers, Dr. Debbie Crews, Léon Foucault, Joel Pearson, H. A. Templeton, Mark Sweeney, and Dr. Carol Dweck. My degree is from the School of Hard Knocks and three decades of coaching, not from a highfalutin graduate program. My advantage is that as a tournament player, I have both yipped putts under pressure and come through in the clutch, and as a coach my simplified understanding of academic research has helped me lead several players from a sense of helpless affliction on the greens to a rediscovery of greatness. If my summations are dumbed down a bit, it's not to diminish the quality of these individuals' research, but to help my students improve as easily as possible. Great coaching not only doesn't have to be complicated, it can't be.

HOW TO TRAIN YOUR EYES FOR STABILITY: THREE-POINTS DRILL

Find a gently breaking six-foot putt on the practice green. You'll need a ball, a coin, a tee, and your putter for this exercise. Place the ball on the green. Next, read the putt and mark the line on which you think the putt should start with a coin, about a foot or two in front of the ball. Then, mark where you think the putt will enter the hole, and insert the tee into the lip of the cup on an angle so that it points toward the entry point. (I'm using a training aid called the Putt Pocket by SKLZ to mark the entry point in the photo below, but an angled tee works just as well.) You now have the three critical points for your eyes to scan and focus on: The "ball," the starting-line coin, and the entry-point tee.

Using binocular vision from behind the ball, visualize and connect your three points. Maintain this focus as you walk toward your ball and set

Three-Points Drill: On every putt, focus on the ball, the starting line, and the entry point, scanning your eyes back and forth between all three objects. This is the best way for your brain to know the precise location of the target. Visualizing three points is the only way to properly visualize line and speed. If you only look at two points, you may get the line right, but probably not the speed.

up to it. Slowly turn your head and shift your gaze so that your eyes trace a line from the ball to the coin. Hold for a count, then continue your eye scan to the precise point at which the ball will enter the hole (the tee). Stare at the tee for one to three counts, or until you're certain you're locked onto the target. Next, reverse your eye scan, from the entry point to the coin and back to the ball. Once your eyes settle softly on the ball, make your stroke, reacting to the picture in your mind and maintaining that focus throughout your motion and for a full count after it ends. The drill is finished when you complete five strokes with perfect eye scans and quiet eyes. (If you scanned a right-to-left putt in this training session, switch to a left-to-right putt on the next one.) Not only will this drill give you laser-like focus, it'll train you to calmly stroke putts, as Charley Hoffman and Tom Pernice say, "back and through past your head," which is where your eyes are focused.

The secret power of the Three-Points Drill is the addition of the third point—most drills and most coaches only require you to scan two (usually the ball and the start line). By connecting the ball, start line, and entry point, you're defining not only your line, but also your intended speed, because there's only one speed at which the ball will roll over both points on a breaking putt. If you only look at the ball and the start line, it's extremely difficult to visualize—and produce—the correct speed; putts that start on line can still miss high or low if the speed of the ball is too fast or too slow, respectively. Getting the ball into the hole on breaking putts demands that you match the speed to the line. Likewise, if you only look at the ball and the hole (and ignore the start line), you'll undervalue break and miss disproportionately to the low or "amateur" side of the cup.

Vision Quest

Students often ask what part of the ball they should look at. Dr. Vickers suggests the back, but the research appears to be inconclusive. I've had different students putt well looking at the back of the ball, the top, the target side, and even at a blade of grass in front of the ball with both a hard or a soft focus. The last choice works best for me, but experience tells me that it won't necessarily work for you. Or it might. You'll need to experiment with each to find the one that allows you to execute the correct fundamentals on a consistent basis.

JOURNAL WORK

Now that you've worked through the fundamentals of starting the ball on the correct line, take a moment to write down pertinent technical keys and feels in your journal. Note how far you stand from the ball when you confirm your setup in a mirror, along with any other particulars in your stance. Describe the sensations you feel when you're performing the Suspension-Point, Worm Stability, and Three-Points drills. In no time at all, you should have a bullet-point list of the keys that you'll commit to mastering. Use the example below to help you.

MY PUTTING SOLUTION TECHNICAL KEYS

○ *Stable athletic stance.*

○ *Toe line two putter widths from inside of ball.*

○ *Nose just behind putter.*

○ *Relaxed arms, square shoulders, shaft straight up and down (and pointing at my sternum).*

○ *Suspension-point maintenance: "feel as if my hands and chest work together."*

○ *Quiet eyes, precise three-point scan. I feel most calm looking softly at the top of the ball.*

5

The Feedback Loop—Confirming Your Foundations

The power to perform doesn't come from
knowledge. It comes from execution.

K nowing how to set up and get the ball started on line is an important
first step in becoming a more effective putter. Unfortunately, this
knowledge is useless unless you can actually apply it to your setup and
stroke when you're out on the course.

I learned this valuable lesson from one of the first students to enroll at
my academy at Shadow Ridge Country Club. He was a very successful and
respected entrepreneur, and after helping him work on his putting one
day, I invited him to my office so we could write out his technical keys and
training structure. As we wrote in his journal, he began sharing some of
the secrets to his financial success. At one point he said, "Regardless of
what you're trying to accomplish, James, remember that you can't improve what you can't measure." It resonated with me immediately—just
knowing what to do isn't good enough, and not having a way to confirm
that you're doing what you think you are leaves enormous room for doubt.
Moreover, resting on the laurels of previous success and believing it'll
automatically carry over to future execution often leads to disappointment.

As a player, you need to know with absolute certainty that you can execute to standard before you compete. In other words, everything you deem crucial to performance must be quantifiable. This is as important for mental strength as it is for mechanics—regular confirmation will make you more resilient as your round unfolds. When you miss a putt—and you will miss, because we are all imperfect and putting is difficult—you need to know that your misses are the result of errors in judgment, timing, or commitment. They're temporary. Misses that result from faulty mechanics, on the other hand, are not. These will lead to recurring disappointment.

SIGHTING YOUR "GUN"

I liken this process to what a professional rifleman goes through before a competitive event. He takes time to sight his gun beforehand, so he can't blame it later if and when he happens to miss. Similarly, your first task when starting a new training session is to take five to ten minutes to confirm that your fundamentals are in order and reaffirm your ability to start the ball on line. There will be days when this runs smoothly; other times you'll have to make a small adjustment or two, which will give you your "feel" for the day. Regardless, it's a critical first step, as regular fundamental checkups prevent you from playing with a false sense of confidence or relying on a feel for too long. Great putters realize that fundamentals never change, but the feels for executing them often do.

The type of practice you're going to employ to effectively confirm your putting foundations is called guided block practice, and your goal is to perform these checks as quickly and efficiently as possible. The Suspension-Point, Mirror, and Worm Stability drills from Chapter 4 are great examples of this type of exercise and should make up a good portion of the first part of any practice session. The second part should involve checking the elements that directly affect your ability to start putts on line: stance, aim, path, face angle, and centeredness of hit. Here's where a guided block-practice station comes in handy. A practice station is a practical arrangement of lines and checkpoints that allow you to confirm any setup or stroke fundamental on the spot. Tour pros use them all the time. Some are simple, while others are elaborate. Here are few of my favorites. Experiment with each station until you find the one that works best, or as some of my students have done, develop your own.

Guided Block-Practice Station No. 1: Richard Lee

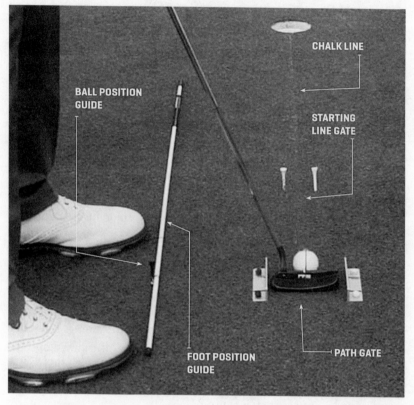

PGA Tour player Richard Lee's guided block-practice station.

In this block-practice station, PGA Tour player Richard Lee has read a putt and snapped a chalk line on the green to mark his aim line to the hole. To confirm that he's starting the ball on the perfect line when he practices, he putts through a ball-width gate that he's created with two tees set about a foot in front of the ball. He's also erected a second gate through which his putter can barely fit to groove a neutral path through impact and sweet-spot contact. An alignment stick helps him confirm that his feet are in the correct position relative to the ball, while a tee marks his ideal distance from it.

With the station in place, Richard completes ten perfect block-training reps, as follows:

1. He aligns the ball to the specific point on the cup that represents his start line.
2. He stands behind the ball and visualizes three points (ball, start line, and entry point).
3. He holds an image of the ball's roll and speed and walks into the putt clear and committed.
4. He engages with the target and makes two practice strokes for speed.
5. He addresses the ball, checking foot position and matching the line on his putter to the line on the ball.
6. He scans his eyes through all three points.
7. He makes a calm, committed, and reactive stroke in which the putter cleanly passes through the rails.
8. He rolls the ball through the tees while keeping his eyes quiet for a full count past impact.

This may sound like a lot, but the entire process takes less than twenty seconds to complete (not including the time required to set up the station), which means that you can finish your block-practice training within six minutes before moving on to the next phase of your training. It doesn't take much time to train effectively as long as you're disciplined and focused. Richard and other players I coach will tell you that I don't get riled very easily. The exception is when a player chooses to train in a half-assed or unfocused manner. Then it gets ugly.

Six minutes—a small investment for such a huge reward. In this small time frame you'll know with 100 percent certainty that your stance is correct, your aim is perfect, your path is neutral, the ball is being struck on the sweet spot of your putter, and the face is returning to square at impact (as evidenced by the ball passing through the tees). That's a ton of confirmation. In addition, you'll run through ten great reps that train your eyes to scan all three targets, communicate where the target is to your brain, and execute your stroke with quiet eyes and a quiet mind. Wow!

Does your current training do all of that? Probably not. I'm sorry, but plopping three balls down on the practice green and rolling putts from the same spot to the same hole without so much as glancing at the break is not effective training. There's no feedback when you practice this way, which means that you can't measure your fundamentals and ability to execute.

Therefore, when you make mistakes, you have no way to learn from and correct them. In fact, you'll end up repeating them.

BONUS: TRAINING YOUR AIMER

Most players, even good ones, often misalign or incorrectly aim their putter, causing good strokes to miss their mark. The good news is that poor aimers aren't doomed to aim poorly forever; your ability to execute this skill is malleable and can be trained. To get it done, your brain and eyes just need some help consistently seeing the truth by assessing the line from two different perspectives with the help of instant feedback. In Richard's execution of a perfect rep during his block station practice, he first sights his start line from behind the ball using binocular vision (step 2) and then views the same image from his setup perspective after aligning his putter (step 6). As he sees how his putter is aligned and then scans down his start line, his eyes and brain retrain to see reality. In my experience, it takes approximately three weeks of consistent work to "retrain your aimer."

Guided Block-Practice Station No. 2: James Sieckmann

The block-practice station I use is quicker to set up than Richard's, so if your time is limited, try this one.

Step 1: On a relatively flat lie, mark the ball's position on the green with a Sharpie and place a dime on the ground two feet in front of it.

Step 2: Measure the ideal distance of your toe line from the ball and mark it with a tee (as determined in the Mirror Drill from the last chapter).

Step 3: Place two ball sleeves slightly wider then putter-width apart on opposite sides of the ball.

Step 4: Roll a few putts over the dime, stopping them in the same spot. Mark this position with a phony hole or tee.

My process for completing a successful rep is identical to the one listed in Richard Lee's block-practice station, but because I don't putt for a living (and neither do you), I end the session after five balls instead of ten. I prefer my setup to Richard's, because laying down a chalk line on the green—

BALL POSITION GUIDE

PHONY HOLE

STROKE PATH GUIDES

My personal guided block-practice station. Quick and dirty—but it works.

and doing it in just the right place—can be difficult and messy. And because I don't use an actual hole, I can use any portion of the practice green or putt with any break. As long as I hit the dime, I know I'm executing the right things, but as I said earlier, every golfer is different. If you prefer Lee's station over mine, I won't be offended. My goal is to make you a better putter, whatever it takes.

Guided Block-Practice Station No. 3:
Dave Pelz Putting Tutor

If you read my first book, *Your Short Game Solution*, you know that Dave Pelz gave me my first coaching job after I decided to quit life as a playing professional. Dave's guided block-practice station makes use of his popular

PELZ TUTOR

BALL POSITION GUIDE

STRING LINE

Guided block-practice station with Pelz Putting Tutor.

Pelz Putting Tutor training aid (pelzgolf.com). The Pelz Tutor is a fantastic learning tool. It uses steel marbles instead of tees to create a gate for the ball to roll through so you can check your ability to start putts on line. If you knock the marble on the left out of place, you know that the putt was pulled; if you dislodge the marble on the right, you know you pushed the putt. A thick, white sight line makes it easy to aim the Tutor in any direction you want, and you can change the width of the marble gate to increase or lessen the challenge.

You can't cheat the Pelz Tutor—either start the ball on line or you'll end up chasing marbles. I'll often set up my practice station using just the Tutor. A lot of golfers putt under a string anchored by two pencils or two tees to check that they're starting the ball on line like I'm doing in the photo on page 65, but I think aids like the Pelz Tutor are much more effective. (If I use a string line, I will almost always do so in tandem with the Pelz Tutor.) My longest-running Tour client, Tom Pernice, Jr., was a big "putt-under-the-string" guy, but the feedback wasn't specific enough (though neither of us knew it at the time), and Tom would commonly push or pull the ball ever so slightly toward the high side of the putt without realizing it. His putting frustrated him for years—we all know the agony of striking a putt dead in the sweet spot and watching it burn the edge or lip out on the "pro" side. When we finally added the Pelz Tutor to his block-practice session, Tom hit the marble on the high side of the putt for two weeks straight. You can't buy that kind of feedback. Eventually, Tom learned how to fight his subconscious tendency to fudge his start lines to the high side and instead commit to the line he selected during his read. He had to feel as though he was going to miss low in order to make a breaking putt. During the final round of the 2014 Charles Schwab Cup Championship on the Champions Tour, Tom drained several clutch breaking putts down the stretch to win and grab his biggest prize check in more than eight years. He looked calm as I watched him on the television screen, but I knew how hard he was battling on the inside. Tom's commitment to process and his desire to work both hard and intelligently is truly an inspiration.

Guided Block-Practice Station No. 4: Julieta Granada

In these photos below, you'll find LPGA Tour player Julieta Granada checking her foundations. She uses a Perfect Path Trainer (eyelinegolf

.com) to create three gates for her putter to travel through. (Her big error is taking the putter back to the inside, which creates contact out toward the toe of the putterface.) Her block-practice station nips both errors in the bud. The Path Trainer also has a cutout line for perfect face alignment, which Julieta marks with a Sharpie. This allows her to quantify her starting line, which she identifies in this example by pegging a tee just beyond the inside right edge of the cup (you can see it if you look closely).

LPGA Tour player Julieta Granada's guided block-practice station.

Although she starts her process by visualizing her three points and walking in with that picture in mind, I added a step where she stands up straight to "stack" her nose over her sternum and belt buckle before she hinges from her hips to settle into her posture. Adding this move into her process ensures that she sets up with her dominant eye two inches behind the ball and with her shoulders square instead of in front and open, which is her most natural position. The alignment rod marks both her ideal distance from the ball (determined in the Mirror Drill) and the perfect ball position relative to her feet.

Julieta is talented and dedicated, and she made great strides during the 2014 LPGA Tour season (the first full year we worked together). Her putting rank climbed from 49th to 7th, and her Tour earnings more than tripled from the year before. Follow her example and you can reap the same rewards.

CREATING YOUR BLOCK-PRACTICE STATION

Ultimately, you need to trust your fundamental mechanics and developed skills in order to free up your stroke and simply react to what you see. However, it's impossible to trust something over time if it shows itself to be unworthy. For experienced players, the work has to come first. Some measure of trust has to be earned.

Open your journal and revisit the list of technical keys you created at the end of Chapter 4. Now that you have a few practical examples of how the pros train for success, follow their lead and experiment with building your own feedback station with the goal of solidifying the critical skill of

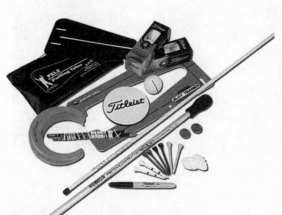

Gather the tools you'll need to build an effective block-practice station and to perform the various drills throughout this book. Whether it's a household item or specifically designed training aid, these tools provide the feedback necessary for you to confirm your fundamentals so you can take them to the next level.

starting the ball on line. Think of the different drills presented in this chapter and the tools you'll need to efficiently—and correctly—measure your execution of each key. Many of these items are already in your bag (balls, tees, coins, etc.), but a few (alignment sticks, training aids) may require a trip to your local golf retailer or e-commerce store. For the tech geeks out there, visit www.blastmotion.com/products/golf or the site I most commonly use, www.eyelinegolf.com.

Keep in mind that your guided block-practice station will likely evolve as you learn or grow in your practice. In the meantime, kick-start your improvement by investing about ten minutes per training day drilling your foundations until you execute them consistently enough to "win the station" (a 70 to 80 percent success rate over ten minutes of practice). In my experience, it takes two to three weeks for your old motor pattern to evolve into a new one that produces consistent results. Be fair to yourself—stay patient and give it time.

JOURNAL WORK

My Block Practice—

○ Towel Stability Drill (one minute)
○ Suspension-Point Drill (one minute)
○ Practice Station: guided feedback for starting the ball on line and confirming setup (eight minutes)
○ Tutor with gate for putter path
○ Tee to mark distance from the ball
○ Alignment stick for foot placement

Expert at Work! Watch me run through a sample block practice station session to check my foundations in a special video at jsegolfacademy .com/index.php/james-foundation-check.

Skill 2: Green-Reading Facts and Processes

Starting the ball on line does little good if you can't predict the correct line to begin with, and unfortunately, it's a skill most players aren't very good at.

I spend a significant portion of most days watching people roll putts, and it's been this way for twenty straight years. As you might imagine, I've seen it all—a constant variety of motions, both good and bad. Every player is unique, and the differences in body type and function, ingrained motor programs, physical and mental experiences, and personality make sorting through it all both challenging and fun. My vantage point and objectivity often allow me to notice the small things in players' strokes that are hidden even to them. But despite this melting pot of motions, there are several commonalities, one of which truly defies logic: Most amateur players have no idea how much putts actually break, even after hitting them.

Take the following example:

Me: "Read this putt and tell me your strategy."
Student: "I read it as a little left-to-right, so I'm going to aim at the left edge of the cup."
At this point I'm thinking, "I'd play more break," but of course I say nothing. The student strikes a pretty good putt on their stated

line or even a bit higher, but the ball breaks across the hole and misses low.

Student: "I pushed it."

Me: "Slow down a second. That's *not* what happened. You hit a nice putt, it just broke more than you thought it was going to. Pushing the putt wasn't the problem. Judging the break was."

The above exchange is extremely typical. Most amateurs blame misses on mechanics, not reads, which is a huge roadblock to long-term success. Poor results and our innate desire for immediate success tempt many of us to fiddle with our method instead of digging deeper. We search without any direct knowledge regarding how our changes impact the individual variables that affect skill, which is a well-worn path into the wilderness. For the player in the above exchange, the real issue is that "he doesn't know that he doesn't know" how to read greens.

One of the strengths of my putting system is that once you prove to yourself that you have the skill to start the ball on line—whether it's simply hitting the coin in the 25-Ball Dime Test or using one of the training confirmations in Chapter 5—you're free from second-guessing your stroke fundamentals after a miss (unless a painfully obvious pattern arises). From now on, when you miss a putt, the blame falls on either your judgment about the read, the energy transferred to the ball at impact, or the process you went through that did or did not allow complete focus and commitment.

THE PHYSICS OF ROLL

There are some hardcore physics at work as your ball traverses the green, so it's best to consult science to gain a better understanding of break— undisputed facts will make you a better green-reader. This foundational understanding expedites the learning process and takes the mystery out of this important skill. At the end of the day, however, green-reading is an art. Beyond accounting for the slope and speed, you have to be able to sense the appropriate line and matching energy for the putt at hand, which may be influenced by other factors, such as wind, grain (the direction in which the grass is growing), the moisture content of the green, and how you feel physically and emotionally at the moment. In short, to be an exceptionally skilled green-reader, you need to embrace both worlds. The first order of business is to understand the basic science behind why balls roll the way they do. Then you can move on to the art: the touch, feel, and creativity that expert green-reading demands.

THE SCIENCE OF GREEN-READING

The scientific approach to green-reading began in earnest in 1984, when a United States Air Force colonel with a passion for golf, H. A. Templeton, showed in a self-published book entitled *Vector Putting* how two variables, gravity and friction (green speed), could be used to compute break on a green. The motivation for his groundbreaking research—beyond helping his own game—was to create a computer model that television networks could use to predict the break of putts, which he felt would make telecasts more interesting to watch. Considering the state of the computer technology available to him at the time, this was a monumental task. Clearly, he was ahead of his time.

Decades later, Mark Sweeney, the founder of AimPoint Technologies, applied modern computer standards to Templeton's discoveries, then partnered with the Golf Channel to use predictive putt technology to power a live graphical insertion of an optimal putt overlay into their broadcasts starting in 2007. If you've seen AimPoint's predictive putt technology in action, you know its calculations are very accurate. But because it relied on precise laser measurements of the greens as well as speed and slope charts, it was, in my opinion, too complicated and time-consuming to be useful for all but elite players. Subsequently, Sweeney developed a more practical way to implement his scientific approach called AimPoint Express. Personally, I'm a fan; anything that's simple to use and helps players at any level improve their skill is a winner.

I'm not a certified Vector Putting or AimPoint Express teacher, and I don't feel the need to elaborate much on either method except to share some basic facts that I think you'll find helpful. If you're interested in learning more about their methods, a quick Internet search will yield a long list of PGA professionals who are certified and would be glad to help. My interest is solely to open your eyes to a few undisputable green-reading facts discerned from science that you can implement into an artistic process in order to improve your skill. It's a process that I've shared with all my

Tour clients, and I'm confident it will help you as much as it has helped them—probably more.

GREEN-READING FACTS

Thanks to research by Templeton, Sweeney, and others, golfers can now separate fact from fiction when it comes to understanding roll.

Fact No. 1: On any planar surface (with the slope only in one direction), every putt that starts the same distance from the hole shares a common aim point. Rolling your putt at this point with the correct speed will result in a make, regardless of where the ball lies on the green.

To find that one point, imagine you're putting on an oversized pool table raised up on one end (creating a two-degree slope) with a hole cut in the middle. In this scenario, on a green of average speed, read the putt for a ball sitting by the side pocket, taking into account two factors: the

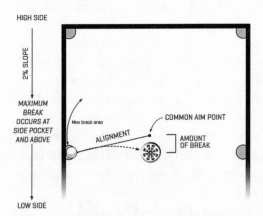

HIGH SIDE

2% SLOPE

MAXIMUM BREAK OCCURS AT SIDE POCKET AND ABOVE

Max break area

ALIGNMENT

COMMON AIM POINT

AMOUNT OF BREAK

LOW SIDE

Fact 1: There's only one aim point for all putts of the same distance on a planar surface.

amount of tilt (slope) and speed of the table. Whatever point you align to above the cup from this position is the same point you'd align to from any other location on the table of equal distance.

Fact No. 2: The more the putting surface is tilted, the higher the common aim points shifts above the hole, and vice versa.

This is a no-brainer. The greater the slope, the greater the break.

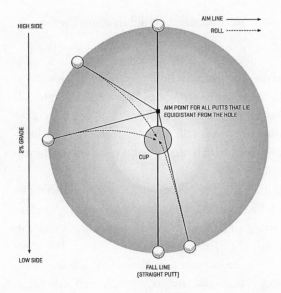

HIGH SIDE

AIM LINE

ROLL

2% GRADE

AIM POINT FOR ALL PUTTS THAT LIE
EQUIDISTANT FROM THE HOLE

CUP

LOW SIDE

FALL LINE
(STRAIGHT PUTT)

Once you determine the aim point, you can use it for all remaining putts (I've shown five, but picture hundreds). If you hit the putt with the correct speed on pure surface conditions, it *has* to go in.

Fact No. 3: The faster the green (the less friction acting on the ball to hold it on line), the more you must move the aim point toward the high end of the slope.

Picture the Masters. Putts hit on Augusta National's greens break dramatically, partly because the putting surfaces during tournament week run so fast.

Downhill putts (because they're faster) break a bit more than uphill putts across the same grade, so on extremely fast greens (with less friction) the area where maximum break occurs moves slightly uphill (up to thirty degrees) above the side pocket.

Fact No. 4: There are at least two "fall lines" on every green. Balls putted from anywhere on these lines must start at the middle of the hole to go in. In our pool table example, the fall lines are directly north and south of the cup.

In the real world these lines curve or meander with the slope, but the overall read for balls resting on them remains straight.

Fact No. 5: Maximum break generally occurs when your ball lies directly between neighboring fall lines. going back to the pool table example, maximum break occurs at or slightly above the side pockets.

On a true planar surface, anything pin high is going to break a lot.

Knowing these five facts will enhance what you see and feel and will help you make sense of why balls roll the way they do. Of course, greens are rarely perfect planar surfaces—they roll, flatten out, and change direction at the fancy of the architect, which requires you to add a good measure of feel to your reads.

There are two additional variables beyond slope and speed that can influence the roll of a ball: the grain (direction in which the grass lies) and the wind. The strength and influence of the grain is species-dependent. On bent-grass greens, which are common in colder climates, the grain tends to influence speed more than it does line. With Bermuda and other thicker-blade grasses, the effects on line are greater, although still not as prominent as the effect on speed. Improved green-maintenance processes and equipment have reduced grain's effect on the ball's roll in general, which has removed a layer of judgment. You're lucky. When I played on the Asian Golf Circuit from 1989 to 1993, courses such as Wack Wack Golf & Country Club outside Manila featured grain so strong it could literally "push" putts up a slight slope. This made choosing the correct line extremely difficult, especially for a guy who grew up putting in Nebraska.

Regardless, my advice is to think mainly in terms of speed, not line, when assessing grain. Look down the line of your putt and determine if the grass looks shiny or dark in hue. If it's shiny, you're putting down-grain—the putt will be fast and break more. If the grass looks darker in color or flat, you're putting into the grain, and the ball will stop more quickly and break less (and break late).

Wind, on the other hand, can have a much more dramatic effect on line. My testing with the Perfect Putter (pictured opposite) indicates that a 20 mph crosswind can move the ball up to four inches on a straight 20-foot putt on a green measuring 11 on the Stimpmeter. That's almost a full cup! My studies also show that the faster the speed of the green (that is, the less friction there is), the more dramatic the wind effect. Of course, you should also account for the wind's effect on speed, which can be significant, especially if the greens are fast. Note that if the grain, wind, and slope are all going in the same direction, the overall effect is tripled. Expect the ball to move a lot!

Rolling balls on the green with the Perfect Putter. Objective tests like these make discerning break easy and fun.

Clearly, there's a lot to consider when predicting the line of a putt, including how you feel at the moment, which ultimately makes the act of green-reading an artful exercise. Science is a solid base, but in the end, sensing just how much break to play is a right-brain activity—there is definitely need for added touch and feel. The question is, how do you learn art?

THE ART OF GREEN-READING

If the thought of assembling all of the pieces of the green-reading puzzle sounds daunting, you should feel even more confident. The fact that it's difficult means that most players won't make the effort to master it, giving you a competitive advantage when you apply these concepts correctly and consistently. Second, I believe meaningful learning is self-learning, and that it ultimately takes place in the subconscious. I don't want you overthinking or "doing math" on the greens—I want you to react to what you see and feel. Tom Pernice, Jr. and Brad Faxon could easily recite the scientific facts of green-reading, but that's not what makes them great. Elite green-readers can simply sense what's required, nothing more. Michelangelo was a great scientist, and he used that knowledge to enhance his art, but he didn't paint by numbers.

Skills develop incrementally over time, not all at once. This one's no different. Any incremental improvement in your ability to see and feel putting lines as an artist will show up on your scorecard. Growth is the key, not perfection.

HOW TO BUILD AN EFFECTIVE GREEN-READING PROCESS

Every shot needs a process—an action plan that takes you from clueless-ness to a clear and committed strategy that gets you ready to play. On the putting green, you'll execute two processes, one that starts when you walk onto the green to determine the break and speed of the putt, and another to keep you focused as you walk into the ball. Your green-reading steps (Process 1) should be organized and well-defined, so that the manner in which you look for and feel the cues that the green yields unfolds in the same order and features the same actions every time. The continuity of this process, along with your base knowledge of green-reading facts, will allow you to improve your green-reading skills with each experience. (We'll get to Process 2 in the next chapter.)

When building your green-reading process, keep in mind that you should read the green or decide on the line only once. As simple as this sounds, it's not common. Many players look from behind the hole and read the putt as right edge, and then walk behind the ball and see the same putt as a cup out. Now what? Clearly this is a bad strategy. A better alternative is to gather facts in a step-by-step fashion until you have all the information you need to read the putt—then read it once. Now you can step in clear and committed to your vision.

If your green-reading cues are defined and accounted for in each step, you won't forget to look and feel for them on any green in any round. The information gathered will allow you to tap into your subconscious instinct and give you a definitive aim line, putt shape, and speed. This continuity is critical. Meaningful experiences build on one another until they become second nature. At some point, you'll simply sense what to do—your subconscious will take over. This is the art of putting.

The following is the green-reading process I teach my Tour clients.

Consider adopting it as your own, or edit it as you see fit. As was the case with building a block-practice station, anything you come up with that works for you works for me.

The *Your Putting Solution* Green-Reading Process

Step 1: As you walk up to the green complex, locate the fall lines. All putts are ultimately straight along this axis.

Step 2: Walk so you can see your upcoming putt from behind the hole. Look at the surface just beyond the cup, and in your mind's eye, place a quarter two feet to the right of your approximate line and a penny two feet to the left. Scan horizontally between the two coins and compare their elevations. Note which coin is lower and by how much. This is the direction the putt will break as it approaches the cup. Reading what happens near the hole first is critical, because this is where the ball will be rolling the slowest and, as a result, where it will be affected the most by the slope. Also, it's harder to see this area around the hole when you're standing behind the ball, because you're at the farthest point from the cup. Many players also make the mistake of looking vertically from the hole to the ball. I like that gaze to be horizontal in nature, from coin to coin.

Step 3: Walk toward your ball and stop at the halfway point between the ball and hole. Did you walk uphill or downhill? If you sensed more pressure under one foot than the other, it's a strong clue that the green is tilting in that direction. "Listen" to your feet—sometimes your eyes can deceive you.

Step 4: Walk behind your ball and picture its speed as it rolls toward the hole. The speed of the ball determines the line and must be considered prior to deciding on an aim point. If you feel like allowing the putt to "crawl" in, then choose a slightly higher line. If you feel like rolling the putt firmly and taking out some of the break, go with a more aggressive line.

Step 5: Squat down and run your eyes horizontally (coin to coin) along the full length of your putt (photo, page 80). Since you've already determined how the putt will behave as it approaches the hole in Step 2, you should have a pretty clear idea about the overall shape as you put the pieces together.

Step 6: If you read any break, gently shift your vantage point toward the low side of the slope until you're looking directly up the start line of the putt. Listen to your subconscious—it will take care of you. Once you decide on a start line, quantify it. You can either point the line on your ball toward the aim point (see below), pick a discernable mark on the green on which to focus your aim, or use the hole as reference (for example, "two cup-widths left of the hole"). I prefer the first two options.

Your green-reading process is complete. Again, this is an example of how many of my Tour students read putts, but don't be afraid to develop your own version. We're all different. The key is that you have one (your competitors don't) and that you stick to it and master it. Continuity will breed success.

The green gives you all the clues you need to dial in the perfect read. Having an organized process to discern them is key to your success.

SHOULD I ALIGN THE BALL TO MY TARGET?

This is an interesting question, and my answer differs depending on your current skill set. If you're a good green-reader (meaning your conscious read is often the correct read), then go for it. Point the line on the ball down your aim line and commit to it. Also, if you're constantly second-guessing your aim, aligning the ball will help you because it removes doubt. However, if you're like most players and your subconscious reads tend to be more accurate than your conscious reads, place your ball down on the green without using a line and feel your way to the correct alignment. You may be best served by lining up your ball on relatively simple short putts and not on longer big breakers, which can require a more intuitive feel.

Since one of the goals of this book is to make you a highly skilled green-reader, at some point you'll be lining up the ball like Tom Pernice, Jr., Tiger Woods, and hundreds of other Tour pros. No need to rush the process. You'll know the time is right when you're passing the 10-Ball Green-Reading Test (page 12) with flying colors. In the meantime, continue to develop your skills.

Aligning your ball to the target line only makes sense if your initial conscious read is consistently correct, or if you tend to second-guess your aiming ability.

GREEN-READING SKILL TRAINING

The effectiveness of your training is the key to unlocking the great green-reader within. To help you develop a training plan, I suggest a mixture of both guided and unguided trials. This combination confirms that what you're doing is correct while also giving you the freedom to grow from your mistakes.

Guided Training

Jump-start your visual training by investing a bit of time with a feedback device that confirms your ability to start the ball on line, such as the Pelz Putting Tutor or similar device (check out the Slot Trainer at eyelinegolf .com), and visualizing your three points from both behind the ball and as you stand at address (page 55). This is a form of developmental ophthalmology, which involves teaching your eyes and your brain to communicate effectively when assessing objects in space. Recall that Tom Pernice, Jr. performs a minimum of ten successful repetitions using the Pelz Tutor for left-to-right, right-to-left, and straight putts on his training days. Even though he reads the green once from each location, he visualizes and walks in on all thirty putts, feeding his brain a steady diet of green-reading truth. The certainty of that truth helps train his eye and build confidence in what he sees.

Unguided Training

You need repetitions without a guide or feedback to train your green-reading process and improve your skill. Don't expect perfection here—this type of training is all about growth. I developed an exercise called the Star Drill to make it easy for you. Here's how it works.

Star Drill

Place five balls randomly around a cup anywhere between three and ten feet from the hole (five points of a star with the cup in the middle). Choose a putt to read, and start your green-reading process (as always) from the opposite side of the cup. Use the green-reading process outlined on page 79 (or your own version) by locating the fall line, then look left and right of your approximate line and imagine the coins on the green to see the late break. Continue your process, choose the line, and stroke the putt. If you miss, don't turn away in disgust or berate yourself. Use the outcome to help you correct your read. Although it's impossible without feedback to know precisely what you did incorrectly, you can make the corrections in a general sense. If you read the putt as "left edge" and it broke across the cup, use a post-shot process to make a positive correction. Begin by revisiting your visual and kinesthetic cues, then internally state the solution, i.e., "a bit more break." Then take a few seconds to reimagine the putt breaking more. The whole process shouldn't take more than a few seconds, but with each repetition, your green-reading skills will grow.

Move on to the next ball in the star and repeat. The great thing about this drill is that there's always a ball lying opposite the hole, so you can get right into the process of reading the next putt with just a few quick steps in one direction. The drill is complete after you've executed your full process for all five putts.

Training in a random fashion such as this emphasizes the "judging" aspect of green-reading—every putt in the Star Drill is different, so you're seeing it for the first time. If you decide to run through more than one repetition of the drill, make sure you do it at a completely different loca-

Unguided practice drills such as the Star Drill are critical to your green-reading development because they best replicate what you'll experience when you play. Here I'm visualizing the late break from the opposite side of the hole as in step 2 of my green-reading process.

tion on the green so you can up the green-reading challenge. The PGA Tour players I coach all make the Star Drill a regular part of their training routine. They know that each green-reading "miss" is an opportunity to learn and grow.

Careful! Whenever you read a putt, don't look for the "apex of the break" as some instructors or high-profile players suggest. Putts often break early, especially those that follow a significant slope, which means you have to start the ball well up the hill from the apex to get the ball to roll over it on its way to the hole. If you only visualize the top of the curve, you're not looking at the correct aim line and you'll probably miss low.

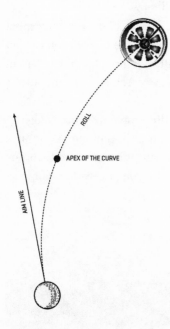

Aiming at the apex of the ball's curve is a popular technique, but it's inherently flawed. As you can tell from this diagram, the correct aim line on a breaking putt points well above the apex of the curve. Looking at the apex instead of down the correct starting line will result in a low miss.

JOURNAL WORK

Open your journal to the Technical Section and add a Green-Reading tab. Write down the basic scientific facts of green reading—just a few key bullet points to cement them into your memory. Then write down the steps in your green-reading process in chronological order, as well your intent in each one. Give every step a clear and a defined purpose.

Skill 3:
Touch and Feel

The short-game skill that most dramatically affects
your ability to score is the ability to consistently
putt the ball at the correct speed.

....

An inability to control putt distance makes scoring next to impossible, especially on "difference-making" putts between eight and 20 feet, which require perfectly matching the line with the appropriate speed. To develop great touch, not only for these putts but from any distance, the first step is to come to terms with what touch actually is, and the best way to do that is to come to terms with what it isn't. Touch *isn't* the ability to hit the ball "hard" or "easy" depending on putt length or slope, yet that's how most recreational players think of it and talk about it. This mentality is rife with fundamental ineptitude, and it's the reason why many golfers struggle with touch and distance control despite obvious talent and years of experience.

A healthier way to think about touch is to imagine the putterhead swinging back and through like a pendulum. (We touched on the dynamics of pendulum motion when discussing the value of maintaining a suspension point in Chapter 4, but it's even more applicable to the skill of touch.) Picture a pendulum in your mind's eye right now—think of a grandfather clock or one of those "perpetual motion" desk toys, and replace the bob (pendulum mass) with your putterhead and the fulcrum arm with your hands, arms, and puttershaft. If you focus hard enough, you'll see that a pendulum:

- Swings back and forth without stopping. (Theoretically, it would swing forever if it weren't for damping.)
- Takes the same amount of time to complete each swing. This period for the bob's oscillation is the same regardless of the length of the overall motion.
- Swings faster or slower depending on the length of the displacement (the backstroke). When the displacement is small, the putterhead moves comparatively slower than when the displacement is large. Although speed changes with displacement, the overall time it takes the bob (putterhead) to complete a full cycle is a constant.

Picturing your stroke as a pendulum and copying its consistent oscillation period means you're putting in rhythm, which is the key technical variable related to distance control. Your rhythm, which is particular to you, never changes regardless of circumstance, which means that the energy transferred to the ball (assuming a solid hit) is dependent solely on the time (period) and the distance of the backstroke (displacement). If that's your picture, the desire to "hit" the ball is completely removed, because your lone directive is to match the length of your stroke to the energy you deem appropriate for the putt at hand and simply let the ball get in the way. Once again, this is the key concept to internalize: regardless of the putt you're facing (uphill, downhill, short, far, fast, slow, etc.), there's one perfect stroke length (made at your rhythm) for every situation. That's touch!

> **TOUCH:** A picture in your mind or a sense of judgment for the perfect length stroke, at rhythm, given the conditions at hand. There's no hitting "hard" or "easy."

IN-STROKE FOUNDATION NO. 3: RHYTHM

We covered the first two in-stroke fundamentals earlier when discussing how to putt on the correct line. But the third fundamental, rhythm, is just as important. Any vibrating object has a resonant frequency, or state, that's coherent and most efficient. This frequency is not only influenced by the length and weight of your putter, but by your whole being (some people like to do things fast, and others like to do things slow). We can define this natural state in several ways, but the one I like best for putting is "a comfortable rate that requires the least amount of muscular effort to swing the putter."

How to Find Your Perfect Rhythm

Matching backstroke and through-stroke lengths is essential to great rhythm and phenomenal touch.

Making continuous periodic swings is the key to finding your natural resonance. Do this: Get into your address position without a ball and swing your putter back and through uninterrupted, mimicking the motion of a pendulum. Make your strokes equal in pace and length on both sides, keeping tabs on how comfortable your stroke feels and the muscular effort that you're exerting to swing the club. After about ten swings or so, slow the putter down to a crawl. Notice how much extra muscular effort this requires. Strange, right? You're actually working harder to swing the club slower. Now speed it up. As it did for the slow swings, this rapid motion requires quite a bit more effort. Pull back on the throttle and look for a rhythm somewhere between these extremes, searching for maximum comfort and minimal muscular tension. After a little trial and error, you'll settle into a pace that requires the least amount of work and feels the most natural. Congratulations! You've found your optimal rhythm.

Now that you've found your rhythm, you need to master it, which you should know by now necessitates quantifying it as well as having a way to ingrain the feel and confirm its execution. The best way to do this is with a metronome, which is a device musicians use to keep time. Both the Apple and Android stores offer dozens of metronome apps for your smartphone, many for free, which makes it a no-brainer. No excuses—download one now.

Rhythm is measured in beats per minute (bpm), and almost all proficient players that I've coached have a putting rhythm that falls within the range of 70 to 85 bpm. Let's assign a bpm value to your resonant rhythm so that you can practice it more easily and effectively. Here's what to do:

Step 1: Start your metronome app, set it to 70 bpm, and lay your phone on the green or the floor.

Step 2: Address the phone as though it's the ball, then take a half step back so you can make swings without hitting it. The position of your phone (metronome) should mark the bottom of your stroke.

Step 3: Begin swinging your putter back and forth to the beat of the metronome, making sure that the putterhead passes in front of the phone on each audible "beep." Keep your stroke equal in both pace and length on both sides of the "ball."

Step 4: Switch the setting on the metronome to 85 bpm and repeat Steps 1 through 3. Now that you've experienced both extremes of the standard rhythm scale, continue changing the beat of the met-

ronome every few swings until it matches the optimal rhythm that
you discovered in the previous drill. Your rhythm is now quanti-
fied. Start a "Touch" tab in the Technical Keys section of your

Swinging naturally at your optimal rhythm takes the least amount of effort
but gives you the maximum benefit when it comes to touch and feel. Master
it by practicing to the beat of a metronome.

journal and note the bpm number. Mine is 78 bpm, while PGA Tour player Charlie Wi's, for example, is 72 bpm.

Using Rhythm to Improve Your Touch

Now that you have your rhythm number, the trick to mastering your touch is to make strokes to the beat of this count while varying your stroke length, and do it comfortably. This is my Resonant Rhythm Drill, which should be a mainstay in the block-practice portion of your training. There are several benefits to performing the drill regularly. First, you can do it just as easily indoors as out, and it takes less than a minute to complete, which means you can improve this foundation during a snowstorm, a mini-break from work, or during a commercial when you're at home watching TV. Second, it ensures that you'll stroke putts at the same rhythm next week, next month, and five years from now, and that continuity—along with the feedback provided by the drill in practice—will allow you to master it. Putting in rhythm will become second nature. Humans are rhythmic creatures, and the beat of the metronome will soak into your subconscious (a phenomenon known as *entrainment*), regulating your whole process so that it becomes smooth, graceful, and unrushed. I told you it was a no-brainer.

The Resonant Rhythm Drill

Set your metronome to your beat and lay it on the ground to mark the bottom of your stroke. Your goal is to make continuous swings with the putterhead passing the metronome on each audible beat. Start with relatively small strokes—think of the energy needed to sink a five-foot putt. Once you're swinging in sync with the beat of the metronome, lengthen your stroke to create the energy required to sink a 15-foot putt, without stopping your motion. Notice how you must pick up the overall pace of your stroke to keep time with the beat of the metronome. After four or five swings at this stroke length, continue the process for a 25-foot putt and then a 40-foot putt. Finish the drill by returning to the stroke pace and length appropriate for the five-footer (think shorter and slower). This whole process should take less than a minute—not bad considering you've just nailed the key technical element that allows for great touch.

The Resonant Rhythm Drill also is a great way to prepare yourself for an upcoming round. In fact, it'll do you a lot more good than slamming a few drives on the range if you're running late for your tee time. Good rhythm affects everything.

Expert at Work! Watch me demonstrate how swinging in rhythm makes distance control intuitive and easy in a special video available at jsegolfacademy.com/index.php/james-metronome.

RHYTHM FAULTS AND FIXES

If you feel uncomfortable when you perform the Resonant Rhythm Drill, or notice that any stroke pace you make in the 70- to 85-bpm range is far different than your normal movement pattern, your current technique for distance control contains one or more of the following fatal rhythm flaws. Nip them in the bud right now! Poor rhythm is one of the most common and destructive errors in putting, and if your rhythm is off, you're adding unnecessary strokes to your score.

Rhythm Error No. 1: Length Rigidity

What It Is: Making the same length backstroke for every putt.

What It Does: Causes the putterhead to decelerate on short putts and creates a "hit" impulse at impact on longer putts, making both distance control and returning the face to square extremely difficult.

The Fix: Try my Color-Coded-Tee Drill.

Grab three sets of tees of varying colors (two white, two yellow, and two black, for example). On the green, mark the start position of your ball with a tee hole or dot it using a Sharpie. Place one tee five inches behind the starting point and just outside your stroke path line (so you don't knock the tee when you putt) and a tee of the same color five inches in front of the starting point. Put two tees of the same color five inches beyond the first two tees, and two more five inches beyond those. Step into your address position and begin making continuous strokes to get into your resonant rhythm. Once you have it down, begin to putt balls from your starting point by stroking from one tee to the same-colored tee. Start with the small stroke and end with the longest. As you roll these putts, note the feel of each swing and the distance the ball travels as a result. Don't worry about the Quiet Eye technique or the line—the goal of this drill is to help you understand the relationship between stroke lengths at rhythm and roll distance for the conditions at hand. The drill is complete after you putt two balls at rhythm for each tee position.

Performing the Color-Coded-Tee drill will train you to understand that because rhythm never changes, energy imparted to the ball at impact is dictated by the length and speed of your backstroke. Prove it by putting "tee-to-tee" for each color code (inset photos)—you'll produce three distinct distances.

Rhythm Error No. 2: Stroke Acceleration

What It Is: Making a backswing that's too slow and short for the situation, and then over-accelerating the putterhead into the ball.

What It Does: Causes poor touch, difficulty returning the face to square, and yipped putts.

The Fix: Try the Luke Donald Drill.

The name of this drill is derived from the fact that almost every Tuesday when I'm out teaching on Tour, I see Luke Donald investing time on the putting green performing this exercise. Place a ball on a fairly flat portion of the practice green between eight and 12 feet from a hole. Push two tees into the ground, one on each side of the equator of the ball and perpendicular to the line of your putt. This "gate" will prohibit the forward motion of the putterhead after impact. Knowing this, think about how much potential energy (length of backstroke) you'll need to roll the ball to the hole with the correct speed. Don't try to "hit and stop" at impact. Relax, make your stroke, and allow the tees to stop your putter. Not only will this drill teach you to make the appropriate-length backstroke to roll

The length of your backstroke—not your forward-stroke—and gravity conspire to create the perfect amount of potential energy for the ball to roll the correct distance. That's what makes the Luke Donald Drill so effective: Because the tees prevent you from adding energy as you anticipate impact, the resultant roll is entirely dependent on the amount of energy you establish at the top of your backstroke. In other words, if you make a backstroke that's too short for the putt you're facing (a common error), the ball won't reach the hole. If you break the tees or push them forward aggressively, you have an unhealthy "hit" impulse at impact.

the ball the correct distance without hitting at it, you'll ingrain the feel of returning the face to square at impact (the face makes contact with both tees at the same time). After five putts through the tees, complete the drill by removing the tees and stroking three more putts with the same stroke length and feel.

IMPLEMENTING RHYTHM INTO YOUR PROCESS

Your process is the ordered steps you go through to get yourself physically and mentally ready to play a shot, and having a great one is critical if you're going to be consistently clear and committed when you execute. For putting, I suggest you follow the green-reading process already laid out for you in Chapter 5, with a few extra steps that will allow you to putt at rhythm. For starters, experiment with each of the following four process examples, then commit to using the one that has the greatest positive impact on both your stroke and results.

Rhythm Process No. 1

After you read the green and create a mental picture of the putt's roll, walk into the ball holding the image in your mind's eye. (We'll add a physical cue to begin your walk into the ball in Chapter 8, but for now let's just worry about the overall process.) Set up just inside the ball, and swivel your head to mentally engage with the target. Begin rehearsing the appropriate-length stroke at rhythm, searching for the swing that your subconscious deems appropriate for the circumstance. (Remember, it's easiest to find your resonant rhythm using continuous, pendulum-like swings.) After you lock in the feel, turn your eyes back to the ball. Align the putterhead behind it and reposition your feet. Scan down the start line to your predicted entry point and then back to the ball, finishing your scan by settling your eyes on your Quiet Eye spot (Chapter 4). Once you're settled, react to the picture of the ball's roll you created during your read and confirmed during your scan, and repeat the swing deemed appropriate by your subconscious during your practice strokes, letting the putterhead swing under and past your eyes.

Process used by: Dozens of PGA Tour players, including Rickie Fowler, Cameron Tringale, and Henrik Stenson.

A Tour-proven rhythm process.

1. Visualize your three points.

2. Walk in clear and committed.

3. Get into your putting posture.

4. Make practice strokes inside the ball with external focus, feeling the required energy.

5. Settle your eyes back to your Quiet Eye spot.

6. React and execute.

Rhythm Process No. 2

Some golfers tend to lose the picture of their start line when they perform their eye scan if they wait until they're next to the ball to begin making practice strokes. If this sounds like you, then alter Rhythm Process No. 1 by taking your rehearsal swings from behind the ball. Again, read the green and create your picture, but instead of walking in toward the ball, get into your putting address position while facing your aim line. This provides a binocular view of the target, which some golfers find helpful. As you look down your line and imagine your putt, start your continuous rhythmic swings and allow your stroke to match the energy deemed appropriate by your subconscious. Now walk in (still maintaining an image of the ball's roll) and immediately align your putterhead to the start line. Set your feet, scan to the target, focus your gaze on your Quiet Eye spot and react.

Used by: PGA Tour player and longtime student Charlie Wi, who finished five of the last six seasons ranked inside the top 25 in putts per round.

If you feel like you lose your starting-line point when you rehearse your stroke standing to the side of the ball, rehearse it from behind the ball while facing the target before you step in to the ball. Make sure to hold the vision of your line in your mind's eye until you complete your stroke.

Rhythm Process Nos. 3 and 4

Some players I coach add an auditory cue to their rhythm process in order to initiate and time their stroke. Once Tom Pernice, Jr. finishes his resonant rhythm practice swings and settles over the ball, he takes one hard look at the target. When he feels ready, he turns his gaze back to the ball and counts out "one" in his head. In rhythm, he looks back at the target on an internal count of "two." On "three" he swivels his head back to the ball and on "four" he settles his eyes. He swings back during "five" and

PERFECT ROLL

Creating the optimal roll is dependent on creating proper impact conditions: returning the shaft to the 90-degree angle established at setup, delivering the putter with a slight ascent angle so that the middle of the putterface contacts the middle of the ball, creating approximately four degrees of effective loft. With great impact, the ball will lift slightly out of any depression and launch horizontally along the ground devoid of spin for several inches before beginning its forward roll toward the target.

PRE-STROKE FUNDAMENTALS

Your setup foundations are the precursor to all movement to follow, and executing them is key to consistency and overall performance. Always check and confirm the following:

1. Your dominant eye is approximately two inches behind the ball.

2. The shaft sits 90 degrees from the horizon (no lean in any direction).

3. Your shoulders are square to your intended start line.

4. Your eyes are over the ball or one inch inside of it.

5. The bottom of your trail hand hangs directly under the ball joint of the same shoulder.

6. You're maintaining a stable athletic stance, with your weight evenly balanced over your arches.

PENDULUM SUSPENSION POINT

Your in-stroke foundations are controlled by the physics of a pendulum. To maintain your suspension point, you must coordinate the movement between all the moving segments so that the butt of the club points at the same place near your sternum from start to finish. Learning this feel is all about feedback; training aids such as the Putting Pendulum Rod allow you to confirm the execution of the above, which builds trust and ultimately frees you up to simply react to the target during actual rounds.

3

4

YOUR STROKE: EVEN LENGTH AND ARCING

A great pendulum stroke is perfectly symmetrical. Notice in the photos how I remain stable as I disassociate my shoulder and chest movement from my hips and spine. My backstroke and through-stroke are even in both pace and length, while my putter swings on a very slight arc with the face remaining square to the path throughout the motion. Returning the putterface to square at impact ensures that all putts start on line. A final key: my gaze remains quiet and I look and feel tension free.

SCAN THREE POINTS

Being able to see and connect three points is the critical information your brain needs to send the ball on your chosen line with the perfect speed. Once over the ball, scan from the ball (point 1) to your start line (point 2) and finally to the entry line of the ball into the hole (point 3). Once you complete this scan, settle your eyes on your Quiet Eye spot and "let it go."

swings through to the finish during "six," maintaining his resonant rhythm on all counts. Tom has putted this way for more than two decades. Not only does counting aid his rhythm, it ensures that he always feels ready when he pulls the trigger.

Charlie Wi uses the words "perfect pace" to the cadence of his internal metronome to time his stroke. These cue words are terrific—they're a positive affirmation of what's about to happen. They're also the correct cadence. Unlike Tom Pernice, Charlie counts a beat to start his backstroke and another to impact, which is why the first word is two syllables and the second word is one syllable. It works because his backstroke is half the distance of his total stroke. If he timed his motion from backstroke to finish like Pernice, he'd use something like "smooth-smooth."

PUTT SPEED AND CAPTURE RATE

Even when armed with an understanding of rhythm and a healthy grasp of touch, many students often ask, "What speed should the ball be traveling as it reaches the hole in order for me to sink the most putts?" Differences in speed (measured in revolutions per second) change the effective size of the hole and your overall make percentage. I could explain this with some complicated math, but the concept is easier to understand with a simple image. Think of the hole as a hungry animal, sitting patiently and wanting nothing more than to capture the ball for dinner once it nears its edge. If the ball is moving so fast that it finishes six feet past the hole on a green of average speed, it's impossible for the critter to pull the ball into the hole even if it travels over its center. Gravity just isn't strong enough in that circumstance to overcome the putt's lateral velocity, making the effective size of the hole zero inches. Conversely, a ball crawling up to the hole with just enough energy to get more than half of it over the edge means it's dinner time. Gravity has its way and the lack of linear speed makes the effective size of the cup its full 4.25 inches.

With these facts in mind, it certainly seems advisable to "die" every putt into the hole, but that's not what you see the pros do on TV. Why? The answer is twofold. First, the judgment and skill needed to control distance within inches is impractical for humans, and the penalty for leaving the putt short of the hole is great. You're better off giving yourself a reasonable margin for error by trying to roll the ball at least six inches past the cup, so that a small error in speed doesn't reduce your chance of making the putt to zero. As the saying goes, "Never up, never in." Secondly, slope and imperfections in the green caused most commonly by footprints—which are most substantial within three feet of the cup—exert greater influence on a slow-moving ball than they do on one moving with some pace. In the real world, when a ball dies just as it reaches the lip of the cup, it tends to fall off quickly to the low side or get bumped agonizingly off line. I always chuckle at the players who react in disbelief when this happens. Surfaces aren't perfect, and if they had rolled the ball up to the hole with a little more speed, it probably would have dropped in, even with the slight reduction in the effective diameter of the cup.

PUTT SPEED STRATEGY AND TRAINING

On any putt, the goal is to find the middle ground between rolling the ball slow enough to keep the effective size of the cup at a maximum and rolling the ball fast enough to minimize bumps in the green. The ideal pace, however, varies depending on the overall speed of the green and the degree of slope. In essence, the perfect speed is one that propels the ball farther past the hole on fast greens and downhill putts than it does on slow greens and uphill putts. Barring extreme situations, here's all you need to remember:

If you're putting on a slow green or uphill, roll the putt with enough speed to make it travel a foot past the hole if it misses.

If you're putting on a fast green or downhill, roll the putt with enough speed to make it travel two feet past the hole if it misses.

PUTT-SPEED TRAINING SOLUTIONS

1. Matching Line and Speed

The truth is, you can hole any breaking putt with at least three different speeds, as long as you pick a start line that matches the speed you've chosen. Distance control is the primary skill, but learning to see the matching line is its bedfellow. To train and improve your matchmaking skill, try PGA Tour player Brad Faxon's Three-Speed Drill. He performs this exercise regularly, and is amazing at it. No wonder he's one of the best putters in the professional game.

Brad Faxon's Three-Speed Drill

Hit the practice green with three balls in hand and choose an eight-foot putt with significant break. The goal is to make three putts from the same place using three different speeds and lines. Roll the first putt with enough speed to make the ball travel four feet past the hole (maximum speed, minimum break). Roll the second putt on a pace that allows it to just drip over the high side of the hole (minimum speed, maximum break). Roll the last putt at your normal "playing" speed, so that it breaks somewhere between the first two putting lines. (To make it easier at first, place a tee on the aim line that indicates your middle-line, normal-speed putt.) Once you make all three putts, switch to the opposite side of the hole and repeat.

Expert at Work! PGA Tour player Brad Faxon demonstrates how he visualizes and works on line and speed in this special video at jsegolfacademy.com/index.php/faxon-three-speeds.

2. Mid-Range Work

When I first started working with PGA Tour player Skip Kendall in 1997, he told me that he putted great inside six feet but hadn't holed a putt over twenty feet in a year. (Perhaps he was exaggerating, but I got his point.) You'd think that if your stroke was good enough to consistently start the ball on line from six feet and in, you'd make your share of putts from any reasonable distance, but it doesn't necessarily work that way. Skip's problem was that he used a slow pace for his backstroke for all putts, which matched well with his ideal rhythm on putts close to the hole, but forced him to lose rhythm on longer ones. Poor rhythm makes touch and returning the face to square at impact difficult, so not only was his touch inconsistent, he was missing his start lines as well.

I consider making mid-range putts a numbers game. If you face ten putts from 15 to 25 feet in a round, and you roll all ten somewhere close to the hole with perfect speed, you'll make more than your fair share. If, on the other hand, you roll only three out of ten with perfect speed, you'll probably get shut out. The solution: Train your touch by regularly performing my 20-Foot Touch Drill. Skip bought into it, and he promptly went on a four-year putting tear.

20-Foot Touch Drill

Find a 20-foot putt with a bit of a slope and mark the starting point with a tee. Do the same on the opposite side of the hole. The goal is to hit ten great-speed putts in a row. A great-speed putt is one that goes in or finishes past the front edge of the cup but no further than a club length past the hole. If you leave a putt short or hit it more than a club length beyond the hole, you have to restart the drill. Roll the first two balls from the first tee and the next two from the second tee, alternating locations every two putts. If you have difficulty rolling ten great-speed putts in a row, simply keep track of the number of attempts it takes you to hit ten total, and log your results in your journal.

(The Two-Hole Knockout Drill from Chapter 2 is another great drill to help you produce ideal speed on every putt.)

BREAKING DOWN THE GREAT RHYTHM DISRUPTER: THE YIPS

A yip—a spasm-like flinch that immediately sends the ball off line and at the wrong speed—is clinically known as an "occupational focal dystonia," and unfortunately, it can't be cured with a subtle change in technique or a slight enhancement of mental skill. The neural pathways used to execute your stroke are permanently damaged. Your only solution, if indeed you have the putting yips, is to change your motor pattern so dramatically that you form new pathways to carry out the act. For decades, many of those afflicted with the yips successfully "started over" by anchoring a long putter to their sternum (or a belly putter to their midsection), which fixed their suspension point and allowed them to feel a pendulum-like rhythm, both proven yip-busters. But since this method has been deemed illegal by the USGA as of January 2016, you'll have to think outside the box.

Consider starting anew by changing to the claw grip, which positions the handle in the crook between your right thumb and forefinger. Positioning your bottom hand like this effectively limits the hinging action of your wrist, creating a fixed point in your stroke and eliminating the right-hand hit impulse. Another idea is to stand on the opposite side of the ball and putt left-handed. Either strategy is a fresh start—a shock to your system that sets the foundation for the creation of all-new neural pathways. Whatever method you choose, work on developing it using the fundamentals, training protocols, and mental keys outlined in this book. Soon, you'll once again feel calm, confident, and competent on the greens. Starting over the right way may actually be an advantage.

If you have a true focal dystonia (the yips), you have no choice but to start over with a completely different grip or putting method than you're using now. This will force you to create and use new neurological pathways to execute the motion.

HOW TO BEAT PERFORMANCE ANXIETY

But before you panic, hold tight—you may not have the yips! Poor putting and uncontrolled flinches are common, but an occupational focal dystonia is not. I would estimate that 90 percent of the golfers that see themselves as having "the yips" have healthy neurology but are suffering from severe performance anxiety brought on by the toxic mix of the wrong stuff: poor technique, poor outcomes over time, and an unhealthy emotional attachment to their results.

It's a self-perpetuating process. Shoddy technique creates poor outcomes relative to known ability and expectation level. Emotionally, these results are embarrassing, and the player internalizes and imprints this embarrassment into their subconscious. Humans are naturally programmed to avoid such events (fight or flight), so when the environment is right for it to recur (similar putt, potential embarrassment looming), a player becomes racked with fear and anxiety. Here we go again! In this physiological state, the subconscious is rendered useless, forcing you to consciously command your body to execute the act. As a result, your natural fluid motion disappears and is replaced by a spastic, herky-jerky one. The more frequent these spasms occur, the more you worry; the more you worry, the more you imprint fear into your subconscious, elevating tension levels to an unbearable high. It's a natural yet vicious cycle, and it often bites the hand of even the most talented players. I understand it. I've lived it, and more importantly, I've helped hundreds of players break the cycle and perform like they know they can.

The solution to putting with greater confidence and trust is multifaceted, but it can be most simply described as "training like an adult and playing with the mind of a child." To wit, children (and any beginning golfer, regardless of age) never hyperventilate over the ball or feel untimely and unwanted muscle contractions, because even though their motor-control and other developed skills are undeveloped, so are their expectations, which makes the results nonthreatening. The rare 10-footer that goes in is an occasion to high-five or dance with joy; missed putts—even short ones—are accepted. The player's self-image is independent of outcome and always tilted toward the positive. They enjoy the act for what it is, embracing the heroic while ignoring the pedestrian. Their healthy perspective and ignorance about the details regarding the "how" of putting leaves their conscious mind quiet and clutter-free. When the "how" is removed, there's only the ball and the hole, rendering the act of putting a simple see-and-do exercise. This is the goal.

Ultimately, your ability to trust your stroke, especially when something is on the line, is dependent on its worthiness. The first step is to make it worthy of your expectation (not perfect), and the second is to re-learn how to let it go and just play. To me that is the definition of the "right stuff."

THE RIGHT STUFF

There are two technical mistakes that directly lead to unwanted muscle contractions during the stroke. To boost your confidence and trust, you must eliminate these before you dive into the mental keys.

The first of these fatal flaws is what I call an "acceleration flinch," which can be best understood, once again, by re-creating the image of a pendulum. As the bob swings back and forth, velocity is least when displacement is greatest; the putterhead is momentarily motionless with a velocity of zero at the end of the backstroke and completion of your forward-stroke, representing potential energy and nothing else. The initial start of the forward-stroke marks the point where maximum acceleration occurs. At the bottom, velocity and kinetic energy reach peak levels, and then the restoring force of gravity slows the velocity back to zero at the finish. Relatively speaking, there's a flat spot of speed surrounding impact in which the putterhead is neither accelerating nor decelerating. I call this the "unbroken zone" of putting, and becoming aware of it is the first step in solving the problem of performance anxiety.

An acceleration flinch occurs when you speed up or slow down the putter in the unbroken zone by changing grip pressure and exerting extra force on the club. The good news is that you've already learned how to relax and swing the putter tension free at optimal rhythm. Rekindle that feeling and refrain from flinching by performing the Resonant Rhythm, Color-Coded-Tee, and Luke Donald drills daily (or as frequently as possible). The Luke Donald drill seems to be especially effective. When the zone around impact remains unbroken by velocity change, your putter will move like a warm knife through butter—smooth, uninterrupted, and flowing.

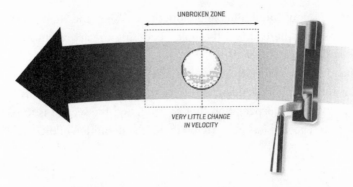

UNBROKEN ZONE

VERY LITTLE CHANGE
IN VELOCITY

As your putter swings through the impact zone, it should be moving rhythmically and at a reasonably constant rate of speed—no acceleration or deceleration allowed. This is the "unbroken zone" of putting. Maintaining it is the key to stopping the flinching in your stroke.

The second fatal technical flaw that creates unwanted muscle contraction near impact has to do with rotation, and it results not from poor rhythm but from incorrect eye movement. As you recall when I introduced the Quiet Eye technique in Chapter 4, your eyes communicate with your brain to provide both the location of the target and the ball in space. When you see putting as nonthreatening and perform in a calm, confident state, efficient eye scans and a calm gaze throughout your stroke are both intuitive and simple to execute. Add in stress and the inability to effectively manage it, however, and everything changes. Under duress, your body experiences approximately 1,200 physiological changes. These changes cause your tension level, self-awareness, and anticipation of outcome to spike, and these in turn begin to alter your eye-movement patterns. If your foveal focus— which is the part of the retina that allows for sharp visual detail—jumps quickly from the ball at setup to the putter during your motion and then back to the ball as you near the moment of truth, a rotational flinch in your hands may result at just the wrong time. (If you're interested in learning more about effectively dealing with the physiology of the stress response, check out the work of Bruce Wilson, M.D.; HeartMath.org, wilsonheartcare.com.)

Rotational flinches are the most debilitating since they tend to misalign the face at impact, causing you to miss from even very short distances. And as you probably know, misses from short range are the toughest to take because you assume they should be easy. A bad result forces you back to the downward-spiraling, self-perpetuating cycle of performance anxiety.

The solution? Improving the Quiet Eye technique described in Chapter 4 as well as creating a mental framework that allows you to execute it. You'll know you're cured when the hole looks big and you can keep your gaze steady without concerted thought or effort in any putting environment.

CHAPTER

8

Skill 4:
The "It" Factor

Having the feeling that any putt you roll is destined to
find the bottom of the cup is the master skill on the greens.
This "It" factor isn't mysticism or reserved for a chosen
few, but is rather a collection of championship attributes
that, with the right direction, any player can
possess, cultivate, and develop.

Putting is a simple act that requires little athleticism. It can be performed equally well by a child, a pro at the top of his or her game, or an ailing senior, which makes it even more aggravating for those who suffer its folly. It's mainly a mental exercise, which explains why the simple act of rolling the ball into the cup has driven many to utter distraction.

We've all heard stories about players "losing their marbles" on the greens. Maybe you have your own personal saga to tell. My favorite took place at Royal St. George's on the southeastern coast of England at the 1985 British Open. Sandy Lyle captured the Claret Jug that year, but most fans remember the event as the one where Peter Jacobsen tackled a streaker on the 18th green during the final round. A bizarre sight, for sure, but not as strange as the actions of South African Tour regular Simon Hobday, who had made it into the Open field that year.

Hobday's play itself was unremarkable (he missed the 36-hole cut). The putter he used for the week, however, was not; the putterhead was battered and bruised beyond recognition. The story goes that Hobday had tied it to the rear bumper of his car following a bout of bad putting at the Lawrence Batley International Golf Classic played at The Belfry in central England the week prior. According to Hobday, the putter needed to be "taught a lesson." (Hobday had first snapped the putter over his knee before tying both pieces to his car.) He dragged the poor misbehaving putter all 198 miles between the Belfry and Royal St. George's. Despite obvious damage, Hobday had the putter head reshafted upon his arrival at the Open and used it that week, only to repeat his abysmal performance on the greens. I assume that, like a petulant child, the putter had failed to learn its lesson.

The lesson, of course, was not the putter's to learn. When you consider the fact that the very best players in the world miss half of their putts from eight feet, and that each missed putt presents an opportunity for self-ridicule, emotional judgment, and a loss of confidence, it takes a mature mental approach to establish and maintain a healthy relationship with your putter. Without one, your experiences on the greens will make performing more difficult, not easier. Although it's impossible to turn back the hands of time and unlearn the process that leads to fear and self-loathing, it's very possible to use reason, knowledge, and self-discipline to reinvent yourself. You have the ability to develop the championship attributes that collectively make up the last essential skill in putting: confidence. As humans, volition (our ability to choose) arms us with the power to fully decide our perspective, attitude, mindset, daily habits, and what we deem important. The ultimate by-product of these choices is the aforementioned "It" factor, which will ultimately allow you to train with the intelligence of an adult but play like a child. If you want the hole to look as big as a bucket and feel engaged and relaxed over the ball, read on.

THE ROOT OF MENTAL PUTTING PROBLEMS

We all enter this world the same way: naked and unburdened by expectation. If we're lucky, parental love and a safe home allow us to maintain this sense of innocence throughout our preschool years. Children do things simply for the sake of doing them, with little sense of outside judgment or opinion.

An example: naked gymnastics. Let me explain. When my daughter was four years old, she went for a playdate with a boy her age down the street. After several hours, the little boy's mother phoned my wife, her voice noticeably uneasy. She reported that she had gone upstairs to check on the kids and found them tumbling, twirling, and laughing with all of their clothes off—performing naked gymnastics. My wife and I thought it was adorable, although we appreciated that the boy's mother demanded they put their clothes back on. What does this have to do with putting? Whatever my daughter's skill level as a gymnast was at that point in time, she was unburdened by expectation, fear of judgment, or inhibition, and she performed up to her athletic potential. Can the same be said about you?

Our loss of innocence starts when we are indoctrinated into the formal education process, which reels in our freedom to do things just for the sake of doing them. Suddenly, we're scrutinized and judged at every turn, whether it's a test score, a behavior, or the way we dress. The social structure of the lunchroom reigns supreme, and our evolution toward typical adult insecurities begins in earnest. The process of feeling judged forces us to consider and appreciate possible outcomes and their social ramifications. We stop thinking in the present and begin to either worry about how things are going to turn out, or fret about things that have already happened. After just a few years of this socialization process, it's no longer okay to play naked gymnastics with your best friend, even if it's innocent fun.

It's a simple yet sinister process. Negative social interactions lead to emotional insecurity, which shape our attitudes and perspective, creating a "warped" reality.

At one point in your life you attempted putts for the pure enjoyment of it; now you attempt putts under perceived threat and duress. "What if I miss?" And because we're programmed to avoid threats through the fight-or-flight response, our palms sweat, our hearts race, our hands tremble, and we approach the ball racked by anxiety.

Of course, there's nothing that takes place on a putting green that's a literal threat. If you strip away the emotion, there's only a ball, a hole, and a simple directive. The goal of this chapter is to help you relearn how to strip putting down to its basic act and eliminate all emotional judgment or consideration of consequence in the process. In other words, the goal is to help you putt like a child. The first step is to understand the genesis of the problem so that you can recognize harmful patterns. After this step, the solution is to choose to develop the six following championship attributes. They are the armor that'll protect you from mental harm and allow you to perform up to your full athletic potential.

CHAMPIONSHIP ATTRIBUTE NO. 1: HEALTHY PERSPECTIVE

Former First Lady Eleanor Roosevelt once said, "No one can make you feel inferior without your consent." The problem, of course, is that most of us have not only consented to let everyone judge us, but somehow we've decided that if we beat ourselves up first when things go wrong, then the barbs slung by others won't hurt as much. You simply can't allow this. Championship putters are consistently building themselves up, not beating themselves down.

The "It" factor starts with the proper perspective and a daily commitment to feed your psyche the positive nutrition it needs to live in the present. You must first realize and then commit to the fact that golf is something that you like to do and not who you are, and that someone's perception of you or your putting outcomes doesn't change the so-called "man in the mirror." Holing a putt doesn't make you a great person, and missing one doesn't mean you're a deadbeat. This perspective will allow you to protect your self-image and remain humble in victory and upbeat in defeat.

Unfortunately, just "knowing it" or "thinking it" isn't good enough; you have to "live it." Here are two exercises you can perform daily to help you maintain a healthy perspective and stay out of your own way.

Affirmations and Neural Linguistic Programming

An affirmation is a positive or encouraging statement you make to yourself: "I love to putt." Neural Linguistic Programming, in simple terms, is the use of a physical cue to bring about a strong positive emotion. It can be something as basic as shrugging your shoulders or a prolonged and deep cleansing breath at the start of your process to remind you to relax and accept the great things about to unfold. Using the two together gives your psyche the daily positive nutrition it needs to start a substantive change.

Begin by defining how you would ideally like to feel over a short putt. Get your journal out, and in the Personal Growth section create an "Affirmations" heading. Write the answer to that question in one or two sentences. Refer to yourself as "I" and write your statement in the present tense, i.e., "I love the challenge that putting presents. I am calm, clear, and committed over the ball." Another example: "The hole looks like a bucket and I'm great at trusting my natural gifts." Be true to your goals. There are no wrong answers here, as long as they're positive and in the present tense. Once you have a few to choose from, find a quiet place where you can sit or lie back. Take a few deep, cleansing breaths—inhale for five to seven seconds through your nose, then exhale for five to seven seconds. (If you can't control your breath, how are you going to control your muscles and emotions when you putt?) After three breaths, use your physical cue to initiate the process and recite your affirmation calmly to yourself twice. As you do this, see yourself living the affirmation and rolling the ball into the heart of the cup. Take a moment to experience the joy and fulfillment you feel, not necessarily because of the result, but because of the way you approached the process. Go back to taking deep breaths and repeat the process a second time to complete the drill. It should take no longer than two minutes to finish. Recite your affirmation three times a day for three weeks.

In my first book, *Your Short Game Solution,* I wrote that one of the main differences between many of the talented pros I work with and most everyone else is that the champion is willing to do whatever it takes to be great. Success doesn't come for free—you have to pay for it. If the steps to greatness feel awkward or uncomfortable, great; challenge equals change. I know more than a few Tour players (Jason Day comes to mind), who diligently work on their breathing and focus daily. If you want to be the "Boss of the Moss" and you're coming from a bad place, you have to be willing to do the little things daily.

Define Your Process

After your neurology begins to rewire, you'll use your deep-breathing pattern and neural linguistic cue not only in daily affirmations, but to start your process when you play. I suggest you start your breathing as you walk up to the green complex and execute your cue just before you walk into the ball. This timing should allow you to closely replicate what you practice during your affirmation exercise.

It's important that your process is completely defined and clear. As you recall, I offered a six-step green-reading process in Chapter 6, and three pre-putt process options that incorporated resonant rhythm and target focus in Chapter 7. Now it's time to finish it off by adding a post-putt process. Combining all three and clearly defining the final product is important for four reasons:

1. Your mind will take comfort in going through the steps in the same order and in the same way each time, leading to both focus and clarity.
2. You'll avoid the tendency to either slow down or rush when pressure mounts. Instead, you'll simply do what you always do: execute your steps one at a time.
3. Focusing on something that you can control helps you stay in the present so you don't try too hard or worry about things you can't control.
4. A clearly defined process can be measured and evaluated, which allows for accountability. Answering for your actions is important for growth.

Your Putting Solution is holistic. When you combine the mastery of simple techniques with daily skill development and a great process, there's no need to worry about results. They are merely by-products of these actions and will take care of themselves.

Evaluating Process and Making It Priority No. 1

Very few PGA Tour players are more inspiring than Ben Crane. Beyond the victories, he's honest, humble, and has a huge, giving heart. One of the

Expert at Work! Watch Ben discuss process and the "Pinnacle of Trust" in this special video at jsegolfacademy.com/index.php/crain-trust.

things I've learned through working with Ben is how to properly evaluate a putt (any shot, really). Most players assess using their emotions based on the result. This is dangerous for your self-image, because bad putts are coming no matter who you are. Ben's approach is much more mature; he ignores emotion and results and instead evaluates and scores the execution of his process using a 1-to-5 scale. If he skips a step or feels doubt or fear, it's a "1." If he focuses on the target, is engrossed in the process, and reacts with complete trust, it's a "5." On the practice green, Ben and I are constantly working on helping him get to a place where all he has to do is trust his natural gifts.

You can't serve two masters. You're either going to pay homage to the results or to the process. Making the process *the most important thing* is a huge benefit, because it allows you to focus intently without "over-trying," or forcing an outcome. Your goal should be to "try" the right amount and not 1 percent more. At my academy at Shadow Ridge, I created a "Process Scorecard" that my students fill out in addition to their regular scorecard when they play. They must post two scores: the total number of strokes it took to complete the round, and the total number of shots they played where they executed their process with intention and conviction (a "4" or "5" on Ben Crane's scale.) Ideally, your process score and your score relative to par should be a perfect match.

	336	553	355	201	440	406	388	517	185	OUT	492	408	168	463	415	156	416	158	502	IN	OUT	TOT
PAR	4	5	4	3	4	4	4	5	3		4	4	3	4	4	3	4	3	5			
HDCP	9	1	13	15	3	7	11	5	17		8	4	18	6	12	16	2	14	10			
STROKES	5	5	5	3	4	6	4	4	4	40	3	4	4	4	5	5	4	3	4	36	40	75
PROCESS SCORE	3	5	3	4	2	1	2	4	4	28	3	4	3	3	2	2	4	3	4	28	28	56

Number of shots per hole where process rated 4 or higher

Your process is one of the few things you can control. By making it the most important thing on every shot and scoring it, you will play in the present and try just the right amount. As your ability to execute the steps of your process improves, so will the results, and soon you won't have to worry about your results at all; they'll take care of themselves.

CHAMPIONSHIP ATTRIBUTE NO. 2: GROWTH MINDSET

In her groundbreaking book *Mindset: The New Psychology of Success*, Stanford University professor and psychologist Carol Dweck, Ph.D., suggests that a person's belief systems regarding their own abilities and potential fuels their behavior and predicts their success. Moreover, the ideal mindset creates motivation and productivity and is a much better predictor of success than talent or intelligence. Even more important to me as a coach of young people is the idea that a changed mindset can have a profound effect on a person's future and career.

There are essentially two mindsets: fixed and growth. In a fixed mindset, people believe that their basic qualities, such as their intelligence and talent, are fixed traits. In a growth mindset, people believe their abilities can be developed through dedication and hard work—brains and talent are just the starting point. This view creates a love of learning and a resilience that's essential for accomplishment. Virtually all successful people have these qualities.

FIXED MINDSET		GROWTH MINDSET
● SOMETHING YOU'RE BORN WITH ● FIXED	SKILLS	● COME FROM HARD WORK ● CAN ALWAYS IMPROVE
● SOMETHING TO AVOID ● COULD REVEAL LACK OF SKILL ● TEND TO GIVE UP EASILY	CHALLENGES	● SHOULD BE EMBRACED ● AN OPPORTUNITY TO GROW ● MORE PERSISTENT
● UNNECESSARY ● SOMETHING YOU DO WHEN YOU ARE NOT GOOD ENOUGH	EFFORT	● ESSENTIAL ● A PATH TO MASTERY
● GET DEFENSIVE ● TAKE IT PERSONALLY	FEEDBACK	● USEFUL ● SOMETHING TO LEARN FROM ● IDENTIFY AREAS TO IMPROVE
● BLAME OTHERS ● GET DISCOURAGED	SETBACKS	● USE AS A WAKE-UP CALL TO WORK HARDER NEXT TIME

A player with a growth mindset sees skills as attainable, not set in stone, and uses motivation to achieve goals. Brains and talent are overrated; improvement starts with hard work and effort. Credit: Trevor Ragan, trainugly.com, adapted from *Mindset: The New Psychology of Success* by Carol Dweck, Ph.D.

As you peruse the table above, look critically at yourself in each category. How do you think and react for each action item? Create a heading in the Personal Growth section in your journal and label it "The Right Stuff." Underneath, make two columns with the labels "Obstacles" and

"Solutions." Next, write down all the roadblocks and pressures you typically feel on the course, and then use a growth mindset to write down a solution for each. Intellectually, you must accept that playing golf is hard and that obstacles are always lying in wait. Embrace them as opportunities to grow, because they're never going away.

In my opinion, the genesis for developing a growth mindset is in having a dream—a long-term vision of what you want to accomplish in the future—and the guts to not let anything or anyone stop you from attaining it. A person with a growth mindset cares little about the emotional judgment of others; only progress matters. As passion fuels your approach, you naturally create resolve, courage, strength of character, fortitude, toughness, tenacity, perseverance, endurance, and resilience—some people call this "grit." When you have it, you'll use obstacles, challenges, and poor shots to direct future actions, not throw a pity party. The obstacles standing in your way aren't roadblocks—they're the road map to success.

Mike Krzyzewski, head coach of the men's basketball team at Duke University, once said, "If you find a road without any obstacles on it, it's probably not worth taking."

This quote captures the growth mindset perfectly. I had the privilege of watching one of Coach K's practices at Cameron Indoor Stadium as he prepared his veteran players and incoming freshman for the start of Duke's 2014–15 championship season—a bucket-list moment for me. Coach K has created a clear culture of growth in his program. Fold into that culture a mixture of hard work, talent, and accountability, and it's not at all surprising that the Blue Devils are perennially relevant.

I've tried hard to establish a similar culture at my academy and with my clients on Tour. I demand that each student react unemotionally to their misses and self-coach by stating the solution in a positive way with zero negative talk. (Of course, I'm there to guide them if they misdiagnose.) We write out technical, training, and mental management keys at the completion of each session. I demand that they endeavor to stay on task and be accountable to the plan by completing homework, scheduling follow-up e-mails, and journaling training results. Many of the Tour players I coach send out an audio report after each tournament round so everyone on the team knows what happened that day and what solutions are to be implemented going forward. We're all in, which is one reason they play so well. Is that the culture you're currently operating in?

Unfortunately, the traditional approach to golf instruction and improvement isn't helping you. It's broken. Golf is the only sport I can think of where players are commonly taught and not coached. To wit, a student shows up for a lesson once in a while, generally when they're at the end of their rope. The teacher tells them everything they're doing wrong from a technical standpoint. They came to the lesson feeling bad about their game and now they feel worse. They leave with concepts on how to improve mechanics, but there's no discussion of mindset, the keys to effective training, mental management, skill development, or structure to keep them accountable. They're paying for a ray of hope and little else.

It's time for all golf professionals to get with the times and establish coaching protocols for performance. I'm happy to report that I'm not the only instructor who feels this way. Many of the coaches I meet on the road, including my fellow *Golf Magazine* Top 100 Teachers in America, *Golf Digest's* 50 Best Teachers, and my friends at the Titleist Performance Institute, are on board. There are also a lot of really great, young, up-and-coming coaches who embrace the growth mindset and are getting great results with their students. The teaching profession is evolving for the better—now's the time for a mature, disciplined approach from the student.

CHAMPIONSHIP ATTRIBUTE NO. 3: POST-SHOT ROUTINE

As mentioned above, one key strategy in employing a growth mindset is having a disciplined and effective post-shot routine. It's a completely mental exercise and should take no more than five seconds. The time directly following the execution of an action is when your self-image is most malleable, which is either really good news or bad news, depending on your mental habits. After you hit a putt, the results will meet your expectations or they won't. The question is, how are you reacting to it and what should you do to grow at the fastest rate?

On a putt that feels great, take ownership of it with a bit of emotion. Give it a fist pump like the Tiger Woods of old, or, if you're not wired that way, just smile. As you do, take a few seconds to embrace what you did well, i.e., "that was great rhythm," "that was a great read," or "I stroked that with great focus and conviction." That's called "imprinting." The ultimate goal after a great putt is to create a high-energy positive emotional state to play in, and regular positive imprints will grow your self-image, increase your confidence, and put a little swagger in your step.

Don't undersell your successes. Embracing positive results seems logical and easy enough, but it's not all that common at the club level. Many of the weekend warriors I coach tend to "ho-hum" their good shots, or even deride themselves despite their good fortune, as in "It's about time I made a putt," "That was lucky," or "If I'd only putted that way last week!" Never self-pity, self-mock, or self-loathe. When you do well, take the credit.

On a putt that feels lousy, the five seconds following your miss are some of the most important you'll have that day, and they can have a profound effect on your career as a golfer. To borrow from the great poet Robert Frost, you can choose a road that leads to sorrow or one that leads to growth and fulfillment, but the right choice isn't necessarily intuitive or easy to discern.

PATH A: THE ONE MORE INVITING

On this path, you choose to embrace your poor results emotionally and wallow in self-pity, whine, bellyache, hang your head, or use the offending club as a tomahawk. Ugly stuff. With this mindset, problems appear impossible to solve as you replay them over and over in your mind. If this describes you, then not only is your future bleak, but you're no fun to play with even if you look like a pro and have a swing to match. This road is fraught with danger, since every round is a roller coaster of emotion and you never know what's around the next corner.

PATH B: THE ONE LESS TRAVELED

On this path, you choose to look at the result unemotionally and use the information you discern to help direct future actions in a positive way. Your first step on this path is to ask "What's the solution?" or "If I had a do over, what would I do differently?" Once you determine the correction, state it in a positive way—"Play more break," "Swing with rhythm," "Maintain my suspension point," or "Run a cleaner process"—and then replay that correction in your mind while visualizing the improved outcome. Then leave it. The shot is over. Don't take it with you to the next shot, the next hole, or to dinner. Focus on the first step of the next shot in your round.

When you choose this path, your poor shots won't cause you to lose confidence or second-guess your mechanics. Instead, they'll help you recommit to your foundational beliefs and use any negative energy produced by the result to steel your resolve for the next putt or swing. Determination born from mistakes is the greatest of all competitive traits. You see it in the face of champions in any sport at the biggest moments. It's the will to win. It's another gear, but it's mental, not physical.

> *Two roads diverged in a wood, and I—*
> *I took the one less traveled by,*
> *And that has made all the difference.*
> FROM "THE ROAD NOT TAKEN" BY ROBERT FROST

The great actress Katharine Hepburn once said that her secret to success was to "never complain or explain," and the same can be said for behavior on the road less taken. The championship mind owes no one an explanation. I recall the late, great Seve Ballesteros's response to a reporter when asked to clarify how he four-putted a hole: "I miss, I miss, I miss, I make."

The inviting path doesn't lend itself to sustained growth or fulfilled potential. One January afternoon a few years back I met up with Champions Tour player Duffy Waldorf to help him get ready for his upcoming season. He had taken some time off, and to be honest, his performance in the first couple of hours of our session was pretty lame—definitely not up to his standards or mine. Through analysis, trial and error, and needed repetitions, his shots gradually improved until he got to a point at the end of the day where he was firing on all cylinders. After the session, as we were writing key concepts into his journal and summing up the day, I told him, "I'm really proud of you for acting like a true pro through the first couple of hours. You didn't bitch and moan, get frustrated or make excuses. You kept your head in it and accepted the bad start as a challenge, and I think that maturity was the key to the day." Duffy replied, "Well, for the most part, those types of players never make it out on Tour—it's a barrier to entry." Then, after a slight pause, he added, "Though I suppose a Scott Hoch or two slips through every once in a while." I literally fell out of the cart I laughed so hard. No offense to Mr. Hoch—if anything it shows how much talent he had, because he was a heck of a player in his prime.

But usually the players who "complain and explain"—as Hoch was famous for—fail to reach great heights.

CHAMPIONSHIP ATTRIBUTE NO. 4:
UNDERSTANDING THAT ATTITUDE SHAPES REALITY

One thing I'm constantly reminded of on Tour is how a player's attitude shapes his or her reality and predicts the future. I may have two different players in the middle of the pack in the Strokes Gained Putting statistic (the same reality), yet one player claims he "hasn't made a putt all year" while the other feels encouraged because he's "stroking it really good." It doesn't take a rocket scientist to predict which of these two players will exhibit resiliency when the inevitable lip-out occurs, or who is more likely to execute with confidence in the big moment.

Fellow PGA Tour coach Sean Foley and I were discussing attitude at a recent tournament, and at one point he offered the following lesson. "Two players are driving to the course in two separate cars. There's more traffic than expected—both are going to be late. Player one becomes stressed, angry, impatient, and aggravated by anyone who pulls into his lane or any extra slowing of traffic. He's obsessed with the negative consequences of his misfortune. At one point, he angrily shakes his fist at a Hells Angel driving between lanes. His attitude has allowed the environment to ruin his day and cloud his judgment. This could end badly.

"Player two, on the other hand, understands his predicament but chooses to focus on a solution. He calls his playing partner to let him know he'll be late and he accepts the environment for what it is: an opportunity to accomplish something he hasn't had time for recently. He decides it's the ideal time to call his mom and tell her how much he loves and appreciates her. The conversation uplifts him—he feels blessed, which makes it easier to tackle the obstacles he'll encounter when he eventually arrives at his destination. Stress-free, he feels ready for the challenge."

Again, it's the same environment for both players, but the attitude of the actor creates a different reality for each. Fortunately, you can choose the attitude you bring to the car ride, and it's the precursor to everything that follows. At the end of the day, we will all meet our maker. How would you like to be remembered by those who love you? Choose to meet obstacles with a positive attitude and change your reality for the better.

CHAMPIONSHIP ATTRIBUTE NO. 5:
EMBRACING THE RISK OF EXCELLENCE

To perform at a high level, you must value and willingly accept the risks required to be excellent more than you value "not failing." Call it "playing with courage," "playing like you don't care," or simply believing in your abilities. In sport, as in life, fortune favors the brave. Think about it: The reward for performing at the top compared to merely playing well is highly disproportionate in golf, whether you're talking about prize money, better playing opportunities, legacy, sponsorship, or scholarship dollars. On the PGA Tour, you could make every cut in a calendar year and lose your card, yet if you can manage just one win, you'll find yourself riding down Magnolia Lane during Masters week with fans praising your name. As such, you have to embrace the risk of going for it and failing as a natural part of being excellent. If you don't, there's someone else who will, and if it's their week, you'll find yourself looking up at them on the leaderboard.

To drive the point home for young players whose parents are usually telling them to "play it safe," I ask them the following question (in front of their parents, when possible). "Do you ever want to three-putt"? The normal response is a quizzical look and a firm "no," but of course it's a trap. The truth is that if you don't suffer the occasional three-putt, then you're not playing aggressively enough to one-putt often, and it takes more than an occasional one-putt to stand apart from the crowd. One-putts need to occur regularly.

Elite putters know that you have to be willing to lose—and know you'll be okay when you do—in order to win.

For those who still don't quite get it, answer this question: If you're playing basketball in a rivalry game and you finish the game with zero fouls, did you play good defense? Obviously, fouling the other team is bad if you look at it through a narrow lens, but from a champion's perspective, it's a necessary part of winning. A player who plays a full game without fouling didn't play aggressively enough to maximize their effect on the outcome. There's obviously a sweet zone of aggressiveness to operate in, but that zone is rarely occupied by the timid.

PGA Tour player Brad Faxon, one of the best putters of the modern era, once told me that during his best putting rounds, he noticed he would finish all 18 holes without a single tap-in. Essentially, every putt was hit so firmly that if it didn't go in (which it did a lot), it went far enough past the hole that he had to mark his ball before he could finish. This isn't a comment on the optimal pace to roll the ball, but rather a testimony to the mindset of a master putter.

Get the Odds in Your Favor

Be bold, not reckless. Certain putts deserve more caution than others, forcing you to alter your definition of success. I suggest you categorize the putts you face like a stoplight: "green" for go (most putts), "yellow" for caution (downhill sliders for example), and "red" for simply cozying the ball up to the hole (you know the situation when you see it). A red-light putt and your subsequent decision to play it safe is a reflection of your prudence, not fear.

Prudence aside, the easiest way to reduce the number of putts it takes you to complete a round is to hit your approach shots into more green-light zones than yellow or red ones, even if it means aiming away from the flag. In my wedge book, *Your Short Game Solution*, I called this "quality position," and it applies to putting as well. A quick study of standard make percentages will help you see the light. Assume that your average make percentage from six feet over the course of a year is exactly 50 percent. That doesn't mean there's a 50 percent chance you'll make every six-footer you face. Some putts are easier than others; for example, you'll probably make more straight uphill putts from six feet than straight downhill ones, or those with substantial break. The table below is a generic illustration of

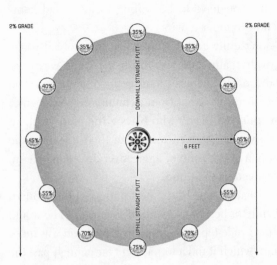

All putts are not equal, even those struck from the same distance. As the make percentages for a six-foot putt by a low-handicap player prove, the more a putt breaks or runs downhill, the less likely the player will make it.

make percentages for a club-level golfer from six feet on a moderately fast green with a significant slope.

From the illustration it's easy to see that downhill breaking putts require more adept judgment and skill as you attempt to match line and speed, which lowers the make percentage. In addition, downhill putts rolling slowly across a bumpy green are much less likely to hold their line. For this reason, when you face a cup location cut on a slope, you'd be wise to value quality position when playing a wedge shot, bunker shot, lag putt, or approach shot into a green. Let's call giving yourself a better than 50 percent chance to convert the putt the "scoring zone." On a green with slope, the scoring zone isn't a circle around the cup as you'd expect, but an oblong oval biased toward the low side of the hole, as shown below.

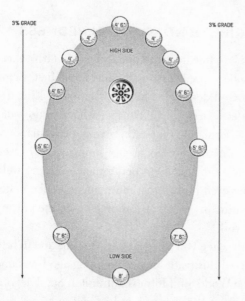

On any sloping green, the area where the expected make percentage is 50 percent or higher is biased toward the low side of the cup. You may be just as likely to hole a straight eight-footer from below the hole as you are a four-foot putt from the high side of the green.

(Note: These pictures are for illustrative purposes only, and do not reflect data for any individual. Actual make percentages differ greatly based on individual skill, stroke tendencies, severity of slope, speed of the greens, and quality of the surface.)

Statistics show that players make a slightly smaller percentage of birdie putts from a given distance than they do when the same putt is for par, and I have heard more than a few academics suggest that this is due to our normal tendency to practice "loss aversion," but I'm not completely sold on the concept. Without proper controls, you can make data suggest almost anything, and as Mark Twain said, "There are lies, damned lies, and statistics." Plus, it's simply a matter of fact that most par putts are easier to make than birdie putts, if only because birdie putts follow longer approach shots, which typically end up in a random pattern around the hole, while par putts are typically preceded by short-game shots, which tend to roll across the green toward the pin and are influenced by slope to end up below the hole more often. I think this is why Jack Nicklaus said that the key to playing Pebble Beach, with its severe back-to-front-sloped Poa annua greens, was being able control your approach shots so that they ended up on the front of every green and below the hole. Valuing quality position puts the odds in your favor!

CHAMPIONSHIP ATTRIBUTE NO. 6: PREPAREDNESS

A major goal with any player is to free up, trust, and let it go, but trust that's sustainable over time has to be earned. The work must come first. Being and feeling prepared allows confident belief to occur naturally. Effective preparation requires a long-term perspective, because what you do today doesn't affect tomorrow's performance, but rather, your performance a month from now. There is no "cramming" for an upcoming event. In fact, the one factor that correlates most directly to performance is to be well-rested, which means that the evening before a tournament, you're better off going to a movie and turning in early than running out to the putting green to get in some "extra work."

You gain confidence only when you pay your dues on time and in full. A recent experience crystalized this truth for me. Not long ago I was one of the keynote speakers at the World Golf Fitness Summit in San Diego, a three-day event attended by more than seven hundred golf, medical, and fitness professionals from around the world. My daughter, who was eighteen at the time and showing interest in a sports-medicine career, made the trip with me, which made for a great couple of days. Waiting for my time to speak, we sat in the audience as former NFL coaching great Dick Vermeil shared the motivational keys he used to lead the St. Louis Rams to victory in Super Bowl XXXIV. Despite no more than a casual glance at my presentation earlier in the week, I felt at ease and confident as I walked onstage, which was a bit surprising because I anticipated being nervous.

Although I don't speak in front of big groups often, I talk and coach short-game performance every day. I live it. And because I "own" my content, I felt completely prepared and comfortable. The words flowed naturally despite following a coaching legend and the intense environment of the summit (I made my daughter proud that day).

Just a week later, I was working with two of my longest-tenured professional clients, Tom Pernice, Jr. and Charlie Wi, at Bear Creek Golf Club in Southern California. After a full morning of short-game practice, we played nine holes. It was a beautiful serene evening—I was playing with good friends with little more than a friendly wager on the line and absolutely nothing to stress out about. But as I addressed a short putt for par on the first hole, I could feel nervous energy entering my mind and body. It's ridiculous—I began playing golf as a three-year-old, competed as a collegian for four years and as a professional for another five, have specialized in the short game for decades and teach putting nearly every day. Shouldn't I have been calm and confident?

No, because knowledge doesn't create confidence. The work you've put in does. The reality as I stood over that short putt at Bear Creek is that I hadn't hit a putt in months, nor invested any meaningful time training in my process, so I wasn't physically or mentally ready to perform. You can't rest on what you've done or what you know. Being prepared is a cumulative by-product of doing the right things the right way every day. The work has to come first. Trust has to be earned.

JOURNAL WORK

Open your journal to the Personal Growth section and write in the six "It" factor traits discussed in this chapter, then make the decision to do the "right stuff" every day. Begin by writing down one simple affirmation about how you can feel, think, and act like a champion for each trait. Example: "I am going to lead the Tour in attitude" or "I love overcoming the obstacles in my way because they lead me down the path of sustainable improvement." Recite them once a day for three weeks.

In the same personal growth area, create a tab with the heading, "Items I Choose to Make Important: My Putting Process." Write out the three stages of your overall process in complete detail. These are the organized steps that allow you to read the green, be confident and engaged, make your stroke a childlike reaction to the target, and grow from the result. Of course, tailor your steps to fit your personality and tendencies. Use the summation of the process that I've laid out for you (Chapters 6–8) as a guide. It should look something like this:

Pre-Putt

1. Begin to cycle deep cleansing breaths as I approach the green and identify the fall lines relative to the cup and ball. Recite my affirmation: "I'm the boss of the greens. I love to putt."
2. Crouch down behind the hole on the opposite side of the ball and scan horizontally (coins) to discern the slope of the last three to four feet of the putt.
3. Walk to the ball side, stop halfway, and use the side view to discern if the putt is uphill or downhill and how much. Use the feels from my feet to help determine the degree of slope—they never lie.
4. Finish the walk and crouch down behind the ball and piece together the first part of the putt using horizontal eye scans. Take note of the shiny and dark hues in the green between the ball and the hole (you've seen the grass from three positions, the grain affecting the putt should be clear). Visualize the intended speed, and if break is detected, shift my body and perspective slowly down the slope and allow my subconscious to choose both a start line and an entry point into the hole, clearly defining my three points.
5. Use my cue to initiate my walk in to the ball and signal my brain that it's "go" time. Stay clear and committed to the chosen strategy.
6. Focus externally and engage with the target. Use the picture of the ball's predicted roll to guide my rehearsal swings, feeling optimal rhythm and appropriate energy.
7. Align the face to the start line and address the ball, scan the three points deliberately, settle eyes on my Quiet Eye spot, and . . .

Your Putt

8. . . . let it go. React subconsciously. Putt back and through past my eyes with a slight awareness of my stroke key and nothing more.

Post-Putt

9. Imprint "That's like me" (good putts) or unemotionally state the solution in a positive way (bad putts) so that I remain committed to my foundations and grow from the experience.

Now own it. Stay in the present and commit to making the process—not your results—the most important thing!

The Art of Effective Training

Combining a high level of understanding with
disciplined, effective training turns the slow
road to skill development into a speedway.

So far in your putting-improvement journey you've learned how to assess your current skill set and demarcate areas for improvement. Within those areas, I've explained the technical and factual foundational knowledge under which you need to operate. The remaining piece of the puzzle—the one that completes your development—is creating an effective training plan to ensure skill development and long-term success on the greens.

Before getting into the hows and whys of training, it's important that you don't confuse the amount of time you invest with hard work—the two don't necessarily correlate. Improvement is fueled by the quality of training, not the quantity. Honestly, if you're not going to approach training with intelligence and discipline, you're better off not practicing at all, because you'll risk ingraining bad habits as well as a loss of confidence. The key to quality training is to clearly define the intent of each session, drill, and repetition. I call it "paying attention to your intention" and it should occupy the forefront of your mind every time you walk out onto the practice green.

The goal of any practice action is to improve one of the four essential skills (starting the ball on line, green-reading, touch, and belief). Within that context, there are only three possible things you can work on: 1) a technical foundation that will allow you to have a better chance to either start the ball on line or control your speed; 2) your ability to read the green and evoke touch; or 3) the mental process that allows you to feel prepared and committed over the ball. Because each of these tasks is different, it should be completely obvious—even to the untrained eye—exactly what you're working on as you do it. Choose a skill, focus on and evaluate it, and then move on to the next. This concentrated effort improves efficiency and creates certainty regarding execution.

MALPRACTICE—THE BANE OF IMPROVEMENT

Inefficient trainers typically fall into one of two camps. The first group is what I like to call the "technicians." These are the players who delude themselves with notions of technical perfection, the existence of "magic bullets" or a putting Excalibur that'll completely change their fortune. When technicians train (and play), technique rules—they rarely pay attention to process and judgment skills. Their lack of wisdom produces streaky successes at best, forcing them to continually move on to the next tip or fix du jour. As they continue to bog themselves down with technical clutter, they fail to master anything and putt worse the harder they work.

The second camp is made up of "putt-and-rakers." They're the ones who plop a handful of balls down on the practice green and mindlessly roll putts without paying any attention to fundamentals or process. They're working on—and accomplishing—nothing. These two futile approaches are the fatal flaws of training, and if you're anything like the players I see daily, there's a very good chance you're following at least one of them.

SEEING PAST THE LIE: PERFORMANCE IN PRACTICE EQUATES TO LEARNING

A few years ago, I started coaching a good college player (she now competes on the LPGA Tour) who putted well except on very short putts. I asked her about her normal training regimen. She told me her college coach made everyone on the team sink 100 three-footers in a row before they could leave practice, and that she hated it. I immediately knew what the problem was—the type of training she was doing was not developing the skills needed to make short putts out on the course when she competed. I changed her practice plan, not her mechanics, and her putting problem disappeared.

You hear a lot about the "100-short-putts-in-practice" routine, and I'm dumbfounded by its popularity. There are so many things wrong with the drill that I don't know where to start. First, it's too difficult to accomplish. A player can hole 65 putts in a row yet feel like a failure with a miss on No. 66. Restarting the drill only to miss again is sure to bring on frustration and other negative emotions. Secondly, it takes too long to accomplish, so there's no time to run a normal pre-putt process, which allows you to rehearse what you do to get ready to putt on the course. In addition, there's zero feedback, so you're ingraining mistakes instead of eliminating them. What exactly are you practicing? Let's see . . . uncertain technique, no feedback, no process to allow for growth, and inevitable frustration. No, thank you.

Trying to make a hundred short putts in a row is an example of block practice used incorrectly. To begin with, a drill like this is wildly inefficient, because rehearsing the same skill over and over fails to imitate what you experience on the course. According to Drs. Richard A. Schmidt and Craig A. Wrisberg in their book *Motor Learning and Performance*, "since the task and goal are exactly the same on each attempt, the learner simply uses the solution generated on early trials in performing the next shot. So [block] practice eliminates the learner's need to solve the problem on every trial and the need to practice the decision-making required when playing golf."

Moreover, the feeling of "greatness" that this kind of block practice creates by design is an illusion, tempting the player to overindulge in mindless drills. With less judgment and skill needed, the results are sure to look and feel impressive, which makes it alluring both to players who want to feel good about themselves and coaches who want to make it seem like progress is being made. Unfortunately, those great results lead to a false sense of competency and confidence—a bubble sure to burst on the course when you face everything except straight-in uphill three-footers. The emotional cost is high, since you're forced to realize that holing those hundreds—perhaps thousands—of short putts in practice meant little.

Because golf is random, your ability to judge and adapt your motor patterns to the situation at hand has more value than the rote memory of a given technique. There's nothing wrong with rolling lots of putts, as long as you simultaneously embrace all the skills required to be great on the greens. Starting the ball on line isn't enough; you must also judge environmental elements such as the wind, grain, and slope to read the green; match the line chosen with the perfect amount of energy (touch); and commit to your strategy and stroke. Again, you need all four skills—not just one or two—to putt well. Given this fact, it's easy to understand why your on-course results may be poor despite bouts of genius during these types of block practice sessions.

Even though training results during random practice—which will make up the majority of your training time during your putting improvement journey—often won't feel as impressive as those generated in blocked practice, the added difficulty of judging each putt separately is desirable and will accelerate your learning and allow you to retain skills longer.

BLOCK VERSUS RANDOM PRACTICE

Despite its diminished transfer value, block practice still plays a significant role for both the beginner and the advanced player, but it's governed by the intent and duration of the session. When you're a beginner or are first learning a new motor pattern, a larger number of repetitions in a safe learning environment is beneficial for establishing new neural pathways and obtaining a certain level of comfort. Because you'll rarely make wholesale changes in your technique, this should also be a rare occurrence and, as stated in Chapter 5, shouldn't last more than three weeks. For an experienced player, block practice serves a different purpose—it's not about learning how to be fundamental but rather to confirm that you are actually executing base fundamentals. In this case, a well-designed block drill can verify that you're executing correctly in less than a minute (one example is checking your setup in a mirror three times before you tee off).

With these truths in mind, ideal training includes both random and block elements, but favors random practice since it better prepares you for what you'll face on the course. I suggest the following:

- Block practice (technical foundational work): 10 to 20 percent of practice time invested.
- Random and variable practice (skill development): 80 to 90 percent of practice time invested.

To ensure the effectiveness of any block-practice drill, it's essential to create a learning environment in which you receive confirmation that you're executing the fundamentals you believe in. In Chapters 3–5, I provided several examples of this when discussing the training methods for building pre-stroke and in-stroke fundamentals, including those that deal with rhythm. The way you feel as you execute may change from time to time, but the actual fundamentals never do. An organized practice station preempts changes in technique that commonly occur without our knowledge or intent. As such, block practice delivers two benefits for the price of one; it helps you establish a feel for the day and certainty that your fundamentals are sound. On playing days, this is huge—confidence in your fundamentals means you can let go of technique and simply trust your abilities.

INTERNAL AND EXTERNAL FOCUS

Block practice can seriously benefit your development, but it requires the right approach to avoid its pitfalls. Many players misconstrue the intent of block practice. Block practice doesn't directly improve skill—it merely sharpens the tools that may help you be skillful. That's a huge difference. More importantly, paying attention to the details of your technique requires you to focus "internally" on each putt, which I define as consciously thinking of a body part in order to set up or move the club a certain way. Although it's true that great players are often buoyed by a simple foundational thought during a round, great putting lies on the other end of the spectrum with "external focus" and subconscious action. There's a difference between having an awareness of a feel and "thinking" about it. The worst thing you can do when you play is to emphasize internal thoughts on how to swing, which means that block practice is training your mind to work in a harmful way. This is another reason why you must limit your block-practice time and prioritize random and variable practice at a ratio of at least seven to one.

When we switch to random practice it's critical to let go of technique, fill your mind with external imagery (outside your body), and attempt to react to your picture of the ball's roll with a "see-and-do" attitude. You're deluding yourself if you think you can invest a lot of time thinking internally about "how" to putt during practice and then flip the switch to think externally when you play. It doesn't work that way. You are what you do most of the time.

Focusing externally is the fast track to mastery, and you have to train for it. To get you started, here are two drills I ask my students to perform to help them create a vivid external focus as well as the mentality to react with a see-and-do attitude.

Hammer-and-Nail Drill

Find a straight, uphill, five-foot putt and set three balls down on the green. Carefully insert a tee into the far lip of the cup; set it parallel to the surface of the green and make sure it points back toward the expected entry point. This is the "nail." Address a ball—this is the hammer you're going to use to drive the nail further into the lip of the cup. Focus on the nail for three seconds, and without turning your gaze back to the ball, immediately get the hammer moving. This drill of putting while looking at the target ensures the action has little to do with technique and everything to do with athleticism and a subconscious reaction to the target. Hammer the nail two more times to complete the drill and purge yourself of internal thoughts.

Charlie Wi's Three-Ball Drill

Obviously, I learned this drill and its benefits from Charlie. On the practice green, set down three balls, pick a hole, read the putt, and imagine it in its entirety. Address the first ball, and then turn just your head to stare at the cup for three seconds. Without rotating your head back to its normal address position, try to make the putt, trusting your eyes to give you the feel for producing the right energy and direction. Next, address the second ball and again turn to stare at the target. Drink deeply. This time, turn your eyes back to the ball, but close them before starting your backstroke, holding the picture of the target in your mind's eye and allowing your subconscious to guide you as you stroke the putt. Guess the result before opening your eyes—this will heighten your senses and awareness of the target. On the last ball, use your normal routine: stare at the target and then settle your eyes on your Quiet Eye spot. Even though you're looking at the ball on this last attempt, you should still be picturing the cup and its expected roll in your mind. Let the putter swing as a reaction to your mental picture.

The goal is to make all three putts feel exactly the same emotionally and physically and eliminate any thoughts of "how" to putt while

Envisioning the ball as a hammer and using it to drive a nail into the back of the cup is external focus at its best. By focusing on the act of hammering, you avoid thinking internally about "how" to putt. You simply react athletically to what you see.

prioritizing the target. This drill is powerful. For some students, knowing how to tap into their athleticism is the only thing they need to elicit positive, long-lasting change.

A QUESTION OF TIME

It should be pretty clear at this point that the key to effective practice isn't total time invested. Discipline is the vital component, and there's a correct way to allocate your time based on what you need to accomplish. If technical deficiencies are making it difficult for you to putt well, then a little science and properly structured block practice is essential. But you must understand that if a little is good, more isn't better—it's worse.

The solution: During block practice, have a clear intent about what you are going to accomplish in a set amount of time. For example: "I'm going to execute ten great repetitions of a fundamental setup, a truthful read of the green, efficient eye scans, and return the face to square at impact in six minutes or less." Note that I said ten, not ten in a row. If it takes you thirteen trials to generate ten successes, then so be it. In golf, you need to give yourself permission to make mistakes. Perfection is a game you simply can't win; it's a path to frustration, not progress. If the success you crave doesn't happen today, take solace in the fact that you're one step closer to finding it tomorrow. Hang in there, focus on confirming fundamentals, and then move on to the important task of developing skill.

RANDOMIZE!

The four skills that determine your putting performance mainly entail focus, feel, and judgment, and the only way to become proficient in these art-based disciplines is to first get your mind right and then do a lot of art. During this phase of your training, varying the environment is critical— each rep you make should entail original judgment and have its own process so that it can be critiqued with a fresh perspective from start to finish. The more random and varied the repetitions, the bigger the opportunity for growth via your post-shot process. Remember, imprint after the good putts and learn from the bad ones. With a mature approach, every outcome becomes capable of directing future actions and improving skill.

This phase of your training can be unstructured as long as there's variety, or organized as a game. Game-based practice closely mimics on-course reality. The pressure of posting a score or beating your buddy increases the focus and intensity of training, and demands that you effectively deal with setbacks and distractions, as you would in real rounds. This gives game-playing a very high transfer value. I challenge both the Tour players and the amateurs I coach to tap into their competitive spirit and "win their way" off every area of the practice facility every training day. I'll introduce some games in the next chapter, but feel free to develop your own. Just make sure they force you to assess each and every putt, have a set time limit, and challenge you just enough to let you win a little more than half the time given your current skill set.

Below is the training guideline I've presented to every player I've coached over the past decade. I believe it to be the correct mix of practice for maximum growth. Use it as your blueprint as you design your own practice plan going forward.

YOUR BALANCED, FOCUSED PRACTICE PLAN

Block Practice: Fundamentals
10 to 20 Percent of Your Daily Dedicated Practice Time

- Pay attention to your intention. What are you going to accomplish in this time frame?
- Put yourself in a learning environment and practice with immediate, accurate, and reliable feedback.
- Own your content. Commit to your foundations.
- Focus internally on simple details: distance from the ball, alignment, ball position, balance, stability, suspension point, rhythm, and Quiet Eye technique.
- Do what's required to affect change, even if it makes you feel uncomfortable.
- Focus on the action, not the result.
- Avoid looking at a target and thinking about mechanics. Hit into open space or remove the ball from the equation when possible.
- Once you have the confirmation you need, quit. More isn't better!

Unstructured, Random and Variable Practice: Skill Development
60 to 70 Percent of Your Daily Dedicated Practice Time

- The goal of this type of training is to learn to get "lost" in the shot and perform the action subconsciously, like you do when you tie your shoes. Embrace the external focus and mental discipline required for this "see-and-do" attitude.
- Practice every variety and length of putt (uphill, downhill, into the grain, down-grain, breaking, straight, short, medium, and long). No do-overs.
- Use your full process, including green-reading for every trial. Practice "trusting" with external focus and full commitment.
- Imagine yourself in tournament situations; take the time to get focused on the target and the shot, and then simply react to what you see.
- Run your full mental program, including post-shot error detection and positive imprinting.

Structured Random Competition: Games
10 to 20 Percent of Your Daily Dedicated Practice Time

- Compete against set goals or other like-minded individuals.
- Win your way off the practice facility by playing simple games like Three in a Row, Tornado, Short, Medium, Long, Brad Faxon's Three-Speed Drill, or Five-Ball 25.
- Play with high-intensity focus and record your results as well as what you've learned in your *Your Putting Solution* journal.

10

Proven and Effective Skill-Training Programs

Before adulthood robbed you of your imagination and burdened you with self-awareness and expectation, you were training to near perfection. The putting green was your Augusta National or U.S. Open, and the putt you faced was to win it all. Other than a bit of foundational work beforehand, you were doing everything right to reach your dreams.

. . . .

Creating your own training program to fit your personality, tendencies, facility, and lifestyle is at the heart of *Your Putting Solution*. Using the perfectly balanced practice guide laid out for you in the previous chapter, your goal now is to design a practice plan based on the results of your skill assessments in Chapter 2, keeping the known tendencies of your stroke in mind. Usually, I try to limit my students' training sessions to a half hour, because it's extremely difficult to maintain a high level of focus beyond that, and "going through the motions" is never allowed.

So what should your half hour of training look like? The balanced guide presented in the previous chapter began with block practice (allowing time to confirm foundations) and then transitioned to random practice (to develop skill). Your half hour of training should follow the same structure. In other words, start by creating certainty with regard to the science of your stroke, and then trust that you have it and focus on the art. To wrap up your session, tap into your competitive spirit and play one of the games described below. Game playing is a great way to get your mind right and to learn to perform under pressure. The transfer value of "winning your way off the green" is sky-high.

PRACTICE GAMES

I've mentioned the importance of games throughout this book, and have even mentioned some by name. Here's a list—and description—of the most effective, but feel free to create your own. Again, a game should have a time limit, should stress at least one of the four essential putting skills, and should be accomplishable and fun.

North, South, East, West

Place four balls on the green, each three feet from the same cup and arranged like the points of a compass. Using your full process, attempt to hole each putt, keeping track of your makes and misses. Repeat the process at four feet and then at five feet, for a total of twelve putts. If you're a competitive player, consider the game won if you can hole ten out of the twelve putts; less-skilled putters should consider eight a victory. Give yourself no more than two chances to win the game per training session. In case you're wondering, the average one-putt percentage from three to five feet on the PGA Tour is 88 percent.

Short, Medium, Long

This game mimics the Long Lag Test in Chapter 2, but adapts well as a game. Place balls approximately 20, 30, and 40 feet from a hole. Lag each ball, and score each attempt as follows:

Hole out: 3 points
Within one club length beyond the hole: 2 points
Within one club length short of the hole: 1 point
More than one club length from the hole: 0 points

Change holes or green location and repeat the process six times for a total of eighteen putts. A winning score for a competitive player is 23 points or greater.

Tornado

Mark six putt locations with coins or tees, starting at two feet away from the hole and then at one-foot intervals after that. Angle the marks so they form a widening curve, which will create a unique read for each putt and an unobstructed path to the hole. Start by making the two-footer, then cycle through the other five putts. The goal? Don't miss. If you do, start over. If you can make six in a row within five restarts, consider the game won. Lesser-skilled players are allowed one mulligan at the five-, six- and seven-foot distances. The best part of this game is its realism—to win the game, you'll have to make a pressure-packed seven-footer.

Games like Tornado, which force you to run through your process on a wide variety of putts with added pressure as you progress, train you to focus intently and perform when it matters most—on the course.

Five-Ball 25

Mark putts at five, 10, 15, 20, and 25 feet from a hole, like the rungs on a ladder. Place a ball at the five-foot mark, two at the 10-foot mark, three at 15, four balls at 20 feet, and five balls at 25. The goal is to make one putt from each distance with the balls allotted, starting with the lone five-footer. If you whiff at any distance, reset the game and start again, giving yourself no more than ten minutes to make a ball from 25 feet.

There's more to this game than rolling putts from different distances—it ingrains the value of one-putting over avoiding a mistake. Champions aren't fearful. They stay and play in the present, think positively, and make putts. Win here and you'll play to win when the putts are for real.

Two-Star

This game's great for green-reading and matching line to speed on the difference-making putts from three to 10 feet. Take five balls and spread them around a hole, creating five random putts between three and 10 feet.

Use your full green-reading process and attempt to make each of the five balls. After one hole is completed, move to a different cup so you can't use previous experience to help you with the read. Changing holes to make it more of a challenge to get the correct read is a desirable difficulty. Set a winning score commensurate with your skill level. The Tour players I coach usually win by making eight of the ten trials. Be fair to yourself.

Three in a Row

As the name suggests, you win this quick and simple game by successfully executing three putts in a row of a certain distance or challenge.

Short Putting: Sink three random putts in a row from seven feet.
Medium-Length Touch Putting: Roll three 20-footers in a row so they come to rest either in the hole or within one club length beyond it.
Long Lag and Short Putting Combination: Play three random holes in a row of 40 feet or more without a three-putt. If you two-putt from beyond 33 feet on Tour, you're gaining strokes on the field. Imagine the gains against your competition.

Up-and-Down 20s

Find two holes on a sloping part of the practice putting green approximately 20 feet apart. Lay down two alignment sticks a club length behind each hole—you'll use these to determine if you hit a putt with too much speed. Place two balls on the green near one of the holes so you're putting straight uphill toward the other hole. Roll both balls and give yourself a point for each putt that travels beyond the hole but stops short of the stick. Give yourself a bonus point in the event of a make. After two successful attempts in a row, putt downhill toward the other hole. If you come up short or hit the stick on these putts, reset your score to zero. Alternate between uphill and downhill putts until you tally 10 points. You can conceivably win this game in as few as five putts—PGA Tour player Nick Watney did it once when I was his short-game coach back in 2013. Stop after ten minutes, whether you win the game or not, and record your score in your journal. You don't need to win every time out. Use your high score as motivation to improve the next time you practice. This is a great game to train for touch and to learn the value of slope or grain, especially if you're on an unfamiliar course.

Big Foot

Start with ten balls and lay the first one down three feet from any hole on the practice green. Continue to place balls on the green at three-foot increments until you reach 30 feet from the hole. Putt each ball, starting with the three-footer. Keep track of your makes, and after your attempt from 30 feet, add the total distance of putts made. A perfect score is 165 $(3 + 6 + 9 + 12 + 15 + 18 + 21 + 24 + 27 + 30)$. Your goal? Set a personal scoring record every time out. This game improves your touch and teaches you to focus on the positive value of making putts.

Drawback

This is a great game that will tighten up both your distance control on longer putts and those critical three- to 10-footers that often turn bad full-swing days into decent scoring days. Choose a random putt on the practice green between 15 and 30 feet from the hole. The goal is to either make the putt or strike it so that it travels beyond the hole but within a club length of the cup (a great speed putt). If your putt finishes with great speed, simply tap it in for your score on the hole; if it doesn't, you receive a one-putter-length distance penalty. Measure one putter length from where your ball lies, draw it back to the new distance and putt until the ball is holed. Your total score for the game is the number of strokes it takes you to play nine random holes. Kevin Chappell, another one of my Tour clients, believes that Drawback is especially effective in preparing him for the stress of competitive rounds.

Reverse Leapfrog

This is a touch game that teaches you how to manage risk, tap into your creativity, and putt with feel. Start by pegging a tee on the green; consider it the horizontal back boundary of an imaginary "distance zone" (you can also use the edge of the green). Lay fifteen balls on the green about 25 feet from the back boundary, then place a coin on the green about 10 feet in front of the balls. The area between the two markers is your zone. The goal of this game is to see how many of the fifteen balls you can roll into the zone without a miss. A miss is defined by a ball that rolls past the far tee, ends up short of the near coin or rolls past the putt that preceded it. Strategically, your intention should be to putt the first ball as near as possible to the far boundary without touching it, and leave each putt about a foot short of the one that came before it—in reverse-leapfrog order. A perfect score would require you to leave all fifteen balls in the zone. Keep track of your high score and aim to improve it each time out.

Seeing how many balls you can roll into a 15-foot distance zone in reverse leapfrog order eliminates all thought of line and shifts focus for touch to a horizontal target. Thinking about the line while you're over the ball is often a distraction that leads to poor feel and speed control, while the right external focus helps touch from every distance.

PRACTICE PLANS AT WORK

If you fix your practice by working efficiently and effectively, your skills will improve and you may indeed live out those childhood dreams of holing putts in the biggest moments. Here are two examples of practice plans to guide you.

Player A:

Assessments passed: 25-Ball Dime Test (starting the ball on line)
Assessments failed: 10-Ball Green-reading and Touch

Training Plan

BLOCK PRACTICE

Drill 1: Hitting the Start Line
Confirm ability to hit your start lines by placing a dime on the green two feet in front of the ball and roll five putts over it. Allow for one miss out of five (three minutes.)

(Any consistent struggles here demand a review of the fundamentals for starting the ball on line in Chapters 3 to 5, and altering the block-practice portion of the training plan.)

Drill 2: Green-reading
Twelve reps of Dot-to-Dot Drill with full eye scans (see page 53; five minutes).

Drill 3: Touch
Swing putter to resonant rhythm beat using a metronome with varying swing lengths (one minute).

RANDOM PRACTICE

Exercise 1: Green-reading and Hitting Start Line
Star Drill with full process to two different holes (five minutes).

Exercise 2: Green-reading and Touch
One-ball putting with full process to nine different holes (five minutes).

GAMES

Game 1: Touch
Short, Medium, Long (seven minutes; see page 137).

Game 2: Green-reading and Mindset
Tornado (five minutes; see page 138).

Player B:

Assessments passed: None
Assessments failed: All

Pre-Steps: Consult journal and take note of the technical deficiencies you experienced while performing the assessments. Set specific goals to improve core stability, rhythm, Quiet Eye technique and the path of the stroke by maintaining your suspension point, allocating your 30 minutes as follows:

BLOCK PRACTICE

Drill 1: Hitting the Start Line
Worm Stability and Suspension-Point drills performed in tandem (one minute).

Drill 2: Touch
Putt to resonant rhythm beat using a metronome varying swing lengths—two sets (one minute).

Drill 3: Hitting the Start Line and Green-reading
Employ Pelz Putting Tutor at six feet and add two ball sleeves to ensure a neutral path and sweet-spot contact. Execute five perfect repetitions for straight, left-to-right, and right-to-left putts, focusing on settling the eyes on the Quiet Eye spot and maintaining a quiet focus for a full second after impact (eight minutes).

RANDOM PRACTICE

Exercise 1: Green-reading, Hitting Start Line, and Grit
Star Drill with dime down on start line employing full process, including post-shot imprinting for one hole (three minutes).

Exercise 2: Green-reading and Touch
One-ball putting with full process for nine different holes with the metronome beating in your back pocket (five minutes).

Exercise 3: External Focus
Perform the Charlie Wi Three-Ball Drill (page 132) for both an uphill, flat, and downhill mid-range putt (five minutes).

Games

GAME 1: TOUCH AND EXTERNAL FOCUS

Up-and-Down 20s—Win a different game every session (seven minute time limit; see page 140).

After completing these drills, exercises, and games, either player can walk away from the practice green confident that their thirty minutes was well invested, because they worked on their foundations and every skill for a manageable duration of time and in an effective manner to maximize benefit. Regardless of the particulars of your training sessions, always make notes in your journal (what you did well, what you learned, what you are going to do about what you learned) and record game results. If this sounds like a lot of work, consider that elite putters such as Tom Pernice, Jr., Ben Crane, Charley Hoffman, Cameron Tringale, and others train like this every day. Sure, putting is part of their job, but it's more of a testament to what's required to be great. And let's be honest—thirty minutes a few days week isn't asking that much. It's a TV sitcom. What's more important to you?

The above examples are the tip of the iceberg; an effective training program can take on thousands of forms depending on what—and who—needs training. As you construct yours, keep in mind that the goal is to master simple foundational elements, a confident subconscious reaction to the target, and the feel and judgment skills of being great on the greens. As long as your training goals meet these criteria, you'll make substantial progress.

Despite the importance of crafting a customized training plan based on your needs, never feel bogged down by its structure—every day is different, and you may not have the luxury of a full half hour every time you train. When time is limited, opt for an abbreviated block-practice session, skip random practice altogether, and play a game instead (win one, actually). This especially makes sense if your time is limited before teeing off, because playing golf is the ultimate form of random training.

JOURNAL ENTRY

Your training program is yours and yours alone. As you construct it, keep in mind that the goal of practicing is to build skill, not look pretty. Train to master simple foundational elements, a clear confident mind, and the feel and judgment skills of green-reading and touch. As long your program hits on these areas, any time you invest practicing is time well invested.

Review your entries in the Assessments and Technical Plan portion of your journal—these are your clues for constructing an effective regimen that emphasizes improving the areas where you need it most. Next, turn to the Training Plan tab and rough out thirty minutes of perfect practice, keeping the optimal ratio of block to random training intact. Worrying if it's perfect the first time out is a mistake. The key is to start the process in an organized, deliberate manner. Your training plan will grow and evolve right along with you.

SAMPLE JOURNAL ENTRY

"My 30-Minute Perfect Practice Plan"

BLOCK PRACTICE

○ *Stability strokes on towel (five reps)*
○ *Suspension-Point Drill (five reps)*
○ *Setup checks with eye scans (ten perfect reps)*
○ *Rhythm strokes to my metronome beat of 78 bpm (thirty seconds)*

RANDOM PRACTICE

○ *Star Drill (two holes)*
○ *One-ball random putting (ten minutes)*

GAME

○ *North, South, East, West (record score in journal)*
○ *Short, Medium, Long Touch Game (record score in journal)*

Tour Confidential— Learning from the Best

When putting performance is the thing that pays the mortgage, it's normal to have a plan that is well thought out and completely dialed in to the skills that matter. Learn from the best to be your best.

The exciting part about coaching the best players in the world is that each week on Tour is a master class in the business of improving. Every day I seem to learn something new as my players go through the self-discovery process of practicing and playing, or sometimes they share something they learned long ago or from another player or coach who has helped them along the way. Players aren't the only professors in this high-level training forum; caddies also provide great insight, because they have the best seat in the house, live their players' performances daily, and see what works and what doesn't under pressure. The reality is that working at Tour events creates an amazing environment to learn and grow. I love my academy at Shadow Ridge Country Club in Omaha, but I realized long ago that leaving "my little patch of grass" now and then was critical to my growth as a coach. I've grown my knowledge and gained wisdom exponentially by paying attention to what many of the Tour players do and why they do it, and it can work the same way for you.

Logically, PGA Tour players' training routines vary based on personality, schedule, foundational beliefs, and an awareness of what they need to prioritize to achieve greatness, as should yours. They don't necessarily "watch the clock," but they do pay attention to their intention, focus intently, and stay disciplined to their improvement plan, as should you. Here are a few examples of how some of the best putters in the world structure their training—this is your inside access to the Tour practice putting green.

TOM PERNICE, JR.'S TRAINING SCHEDULE

Block Practice

- Putting Professor: ten to twenty putts per week (hotel room or on-site; see below).
- Practice Station with Pelz Putting Tutor with aim line (three stations): ten reps on a straight putt, ten reps on a left-to-right putt, and ten reps on a right-to-left. Then, one rep at each station in succession, cycled through three times. Performed on every training day (or three times a week).

Random Practice

- Star Drill (two holes, or as time allows)
- One-Ball Random Putting (nine holes)
- Forty-Fifty-Sixty speed work (ten minutes; see below)

Games

Perform two or three of the following, depending on time commitments:
- Short, Medium, Long
- Up-and-Down 20s
- Three-Hole Knockout
- North, South, East, West

What I Like Most About Tom's Training

Pernice uses an interesting combination of block-practice stations each week to ensure that his fundamentals and feels are sound before he works on touch and process. To re-create his ideal stroke shape, with the shaft staying on the plane that he establishes at setup and the face staying square to it throughout the motion, he trains on a device called the Putting Professor. There are both positives and potential negatives for using a guided device like this. On the positive side, this training aid gives instant feedback and easily allows you to feel and produce the perfect stroke shape time after time, and continuity over a long period of time is one of the keys to mastery.

Tom Pernice, Jr. uses the Putting Professor training aid to consistently re-create his ideal stroke shape (path, face, and ascent/descent angles). Aids like this are ideal for learning a new motor pattern, but to perform your best, you ultimately must focus on skill and be able to execute without a guide.

There are risks with guided devices, however, and Tom and I learned the hard way that tools can distract you and hinder performance if the work isn't properly compartmentalized. Remember that internal thoughts about how to move or control your putter during block practice tend to ruin fluid and athletic movement and generally don't hold up well under duress. On the course, it's advantageous to focus on items that are "freeing," like rhythm, Quiet Eye, and process; consciously trying to reproduce a perfect, aid-guided stroke shape has the opposite effect. Regardless of the devices you use, be disciplined to relegate them to your block practice only and let their positive effects "bleed" into your subconscious over time instead of forcing associated feels when you play.

Over the past year, Tom has prioritized skill over stroke shape in his block practice by confirming the correct read and start line by using a Pelz

Putting Tutor / aim-line combination and cycling through three different putting locations. Being more skill-driven has allowed him to focus externally, which has freed him up, and as a result he's made huge strides in his performance. I love the way he utilizes the Putting Tutor on three putt types, because as imperfect humans, we often change unwittingly, whether it's how we see, feel, or execute the fundamentals. Without proper feedback, downhill right-to-left putts may feel awkward one day, while straight putts may feel awkward the next. Tom's block-practice stations feed him a steady diet of truth on all putt types, which has greatly improved his consistency.

Tom has a great pendulum arc to his swing, and because he has counted and swung his putter to a six count during his routine for the past twenty years, his rhythm is impeccable. Touch, for him, is nothing more than training his eyes to sense the speed of the green and the distance to the hole. To further develop his touch, he finds a downhill putt on the practice green and sets out tees at 40, 50, and 60 feet from the hole (Forty-Fifty-Sixty random speed work). He rolls three lag putts from each tee to the hole, then repeats for an uphill putt by rolling three balls to each tee. He'll often make Forty-Fifty-Sixty a game by putting one additional ball from each location and scoring his results. (In order to proceed from downhill putts to uphill putts, he must roll all three putts to within a club length of the hole, and complete the game by doing likewise on the uphill attempts.) I suggest you set any standard you feel is appropriate for your skill level and play Tom's touch game to win your way off the green.

BEN CRANE'S TRAINING SCHEDULE

Block Practice

- Center Face, Center Ball Drill (five reps once a week; see below)
- Dime Test (Complete five to ten successful rolls over the dime daily)

If he's able to confirm his ability to start the ball on line, Ben moves on to random practice. If not, he performs the . . .

- Black-Line Drill (ten successful putts from three different locations—straight in, right-to-left, and left-to-right; see below)

Random Practice

- One-Ball Random Putting (as time allows)
- Read & Putt (nine holes; see below)

Games

- Two-Star
- Three in a Row

What I like Most About Ben's Training

Ben keeps it simple and to the point. He lays a dime down on the green about four feet away from the ball and uses his eyes and his athleticism to roll putts over it to confirm that he's mastered the skill of starting the ball on line, allowing him to focus his practice efforts elsewhere. For Crane, it's rarely about technique—he's proven over the last decade that he's one of the best putters in the world. If for some reason he feels like he's missing his start lines, he'll calibrate his eyes and ability to aim by performing his Black-Line Drill. This entails setting up three putting stations to the same hole, in which the reads are straight in, a ball outside left, and a ball outside right. He then uses a Sharpie to draw a black line on the green perpendicular to his start line and to mark a dot a foot in front of the ball. At setup, he'll match the leading edge of his putter to the black line to make sure the face is square, then calibrate his eyes by scanning through the dot and into the cup. With the guides in place, it doesn't take long for Ben to rekindle the feels he needs to hit his start line on every type of putt.

After a handful of successful repetitions from each location, he moves on to training his sense of touch, judgment, and process via random practice. Ben views the Black-Line Drill as nothing more than a shooter taking time to sight his gun before hunting. A "sighted gun" instills the confidence he needs to avoid second-guessing his aim or technique on the course when he misses, which makes him resilient and allows him to think about the ball and the target and nothing else.

Read & Putt is essentially random practice with feedback, provided in this case by a video camera, caddie, or trusted friend. With just one ball in hand, select any putt on the practice green of 15 feet or less. Read the putt, then put a tee into the ground on your start line even with or just beyond the cup. Set up your video camera on a tripod behind the ball (or ask your caddie or friend to stand in the same place) and focus the lens so that it can record both your stroke and the putt in full. Read, putt, and record on nine different holes, then review the tape. Video is truth, so watch and learn. You'll discern quite a lot about your ability to read putts correctly, your aim, your stroke shape, and whether you're hitting your start lines. Every player has his or her tendencies, and knowing yours will prove to be a huge advantage. I didn't teach Read & Putt to Ben; one of his former coaches, Carl Welty, did. I love its effectiveness. Anyone can execute with the help of training aids; it's a different story when you're on your own. Your Read & Putt tapes will expose your flaws and tendencies. Use them as blueprints for crafting future training plans that address your specific weaknesses.

Embedded tee

Ben Crane performing his Center-Face, Center-Ball Drill, an effective exercise for players who struggle with catching the ball off the sweet spot by hitting it high on the putterface. To perform this drill, Ben pushes a tee into the ground directly behind the ball so that only the crown is exposed. The goal? Deliver the putterhead to the ball on a slightly ascending angle of attack so that the putter just misses the tee. If you hit the tee, your angle of attack is too steep—you'll make contact above the sweet spot and fail to optimize roll.

CHARLEY HOFFMANN'S TRAINING SCHEDULE

Block Practice

- T-Square on straight putts (two minutes; see below)
- Dot-to-Dot (seven minutes; see below)

Random Practice

- One-Ball Random Putting (five minutes)

Games (As Time Allows)

- Short, Medium, Long
- Two-hole Knockout Test
- Read & Putt (nine holes)

What I like Most About Charley's Training

Charley is not only talented and hardworking, he has the perfect attitude to be an elite performer. He pays attention to the details when he trains his mechanics, but he doesn't let the technical stuff or results affect him on the course. He's a "surfer dude" at heart, which is a huge asset, because it's critical to remain calm when facing pressure or when your "A" game just isn't there. Charley starts the block section of his training by holing ten straight-in four-footers, checking his distance from the ball, ball position, stance, and shoulder and putterface alignment using a T-square in front of a mirror on each one (photo, page 154).

The T-square allows Charley to confirm in just two minutes that he's executing nearly every main pre-stroke fundamental correctly, and because it's both simple and effective, he hasn't strayed from it in the six years I've been coaching him.

He follows up his T-square work with a drill designed to train his eyes to scan down the correct line on breaking putts, called "Dot-to-Dot." I learned this drill from another one of my Tour clients, James Driscoll. Here's how it works: Find a severely breaking short putt and mark the ball's position at address by dotting the green with a Sharpie. Read the putt,

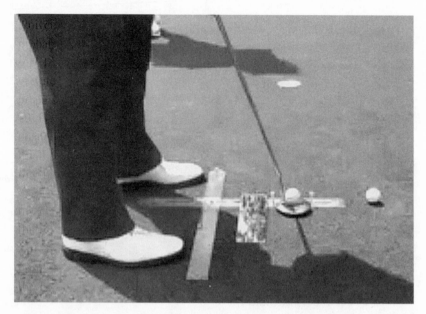

Charley Hoffman uses a T-square to check his pre-stroke fundamentals on straight putts to kick off the block section of his regular training program. Like all elite putters, Charley knows that setting up properly is the key to all the moves that follow and, ultimately, his consistency for starting the ball on his intended line.

choose a starting line to the best of your ability, and mark your starting line by punching a small hole in the green with a tee about 18 inches in front of the first dot. Putt a few balls over the mark and adjust the correct start-line spot based on your results. Once you have the read nailed, mark the starting line with another Sharpie dot. Next, place an alignment stick parallel to the two dots so that you can confirm your stance and aim. It should look like this:

To complete the drill, place a ball on the first dot, then stand behind the ball and visualize three points: the ball (Dot 1), your start line (Dot 2), and the expected entry point into the hole. Holding this picture in your mind's eye, walk in and align your putter to the start line using the stick for confirmation. After settling into your stance, cleanly and efficiently scan your eyes from dot to dot and over the entry point, and then back again. Settle your eyes on your Quiet Eye spot, react to what you see by letting the putter swing back and through past your head, finding and focusing on

Charley Hoffman performing the Dot-to-Dot drill to groove the proper aim fundamentals, as well as efficiently train his eyes to scan three targets.

the dot underneath the ball for a full second before looking up. That's one repetition. Hoffman and Driscoll perform three for both left-to-right and right-to-left putts, and often repeat the cycle in full, which takes them about five to seven minutes.

After completing the Dot-to-Dot drill and a little One-Ball Random Putting, Charley will either win his way off the green playing a touch game or play nine holes of Read & Putt with his caddie, Bret Waldman, acting as the camera.

CHARLIE WI'S TRAINING SCHEDULE

Block Practice

- Putting Arc (three minutes)
- Resonant Rhythm Drill (one minute)
- Metronome work with aim line (three minutes)

Random Practice

- Three-Ball Drill (five minutes)
- One-Ball Random Putting (as time allows)

Games

- Three-Hole Knockout (five minutes)
- Short, Medium, Long (ten minutes)
- Read & Putt (nine holes if time allows)

What I Like Most About Charlie's Training

Charlie is disciplined about using his metronome and training his rhythm every day. We've worked hard on this since I started coaching him two decades ago—that's commitment! The thing I like most about Charlie's practice is that he transitions quickly from the internal focus in his block practice to external focus by performing his Three-Ball Drill. If you can see the target clearly in your mind's eye and react with complete commitment like an athlete, you have a huge advantage over the army of overthinkers you'll compete against. In addition, it'll help you rekindle your childlike approach to putting—free, un-judged, and fearless.

CAMERON TRINGALE'S TRAINING SCHEDULE

Block Practice

- Aim line with gate / Prayer Drill (ten reps)
- Aim line with gate / Normal Grip (ten reps; see below)

Random Practice

- Star Drill (minimum two holes)
- One-Ball Random Putting (distance putts for touch as time allows)

Games

- Three in a Row

What I like Most About Cameron's Training

Cameron's gift as a player is his perspective, attitude, and commitment to process. I hate to say this, because I may live to regret it later, but he's my favorite player to work with for these very reasons. He just doesn't ever seem to get in his own way. Cam opens his block practice by performing the Prayer Drill with an aim-line and gate (see Chapter 4, pages 47–49). The Prayer Drill not only activates the proper muscles and coordinates their movement so that the player's suspension point is maintained, it also creates the feelings of connection and free-flowing rhythm, which Cameron loves. After creating the sensation, and he rekindles it using his normal grip.

Cameron Tringale confirms his setup alignments, stroke shape and suspension point with a simple but effective feedback station, first using a "prayer" grip followed immediately with his usual hold. It takes him just a few minutes to confirm that he's executing all the technical foundations of his plan.

Following this block-practice sequence, his training schedule is mostly about process—training his pre-, in- and post-stroke steps to build trust and let the results take care of themselves.

Expert at Work! Watch Cameron Tringale perform the Prayer Drill and explain its benefits in a special video at jsegolfacademy.com/index.php/cameron-prayer.

JOURNAL WORK

At this point, you know just about everything I know about putting and training—you're ready to finalize your PGA Tour–level practice program. Open your journal to the first page and revisit your stated goals. Your passion for achieving them will serve as the driving force for you to pay attention to the details as you work both hard and smart. Turn to the "Training" tab in your journal and review the roughed-out version you created after reading Chapter 10. Review your notes, consider what the best players in the world do to stay organized and on point, and make final adjustments, if needed. You're ready to train like a pro.

PARTING THOUGHTS

Whew! That was a lot of information, but the goal of *Your Putting Solution* was to arm you with everything you need to dramatically improve your putting in the absence of lingering doubts or unanswered questions about what you need to do to change your fortune on the greens. If you boil it all down to a quest to grow the four essential skills, and see your organized half-hour practice sessions and mental exercises as the means to get it done, it's a fairly uncomplicated process. *You can do this!*

I've helped hundreds—if not a thousand—players sift through this process, organize their thoughts and actions, and improve their putting performances beyond what even they thought was possible. It simply takes a willingness to do the right kind of work. You can't think that the tasks of affirming your skills or journaling are "silly," or that training your eyes to be "quiet" and scan a precise line is mental hocus-pocus. Nor can you scrap your foundations for fads or "the next big thing" after one bad putting round. Stay strong, remain committed, and endeavor to improve every time you practice and play. Magic bullets do not exist.

If you've read this far, you know what the solutions are, and that there will be obstacles in your path that can either push you forward or derail you, pending your perspective and mindset. I'm optimistic that you'll get the job done. Personal growth derived from wisdom and self-discipline is near the top of the best things you can experience in life.

This is a journey worth taking. Enjoy it.